This volume was subsidized by the open fund of key laboratory for road engineering in permafrost regions of CCCC First Highway Consultants Co., Ltd.

中交第一公路勘察设计研究院有限公司
中交寒区道路工程重点实验室开放基金 资助项目

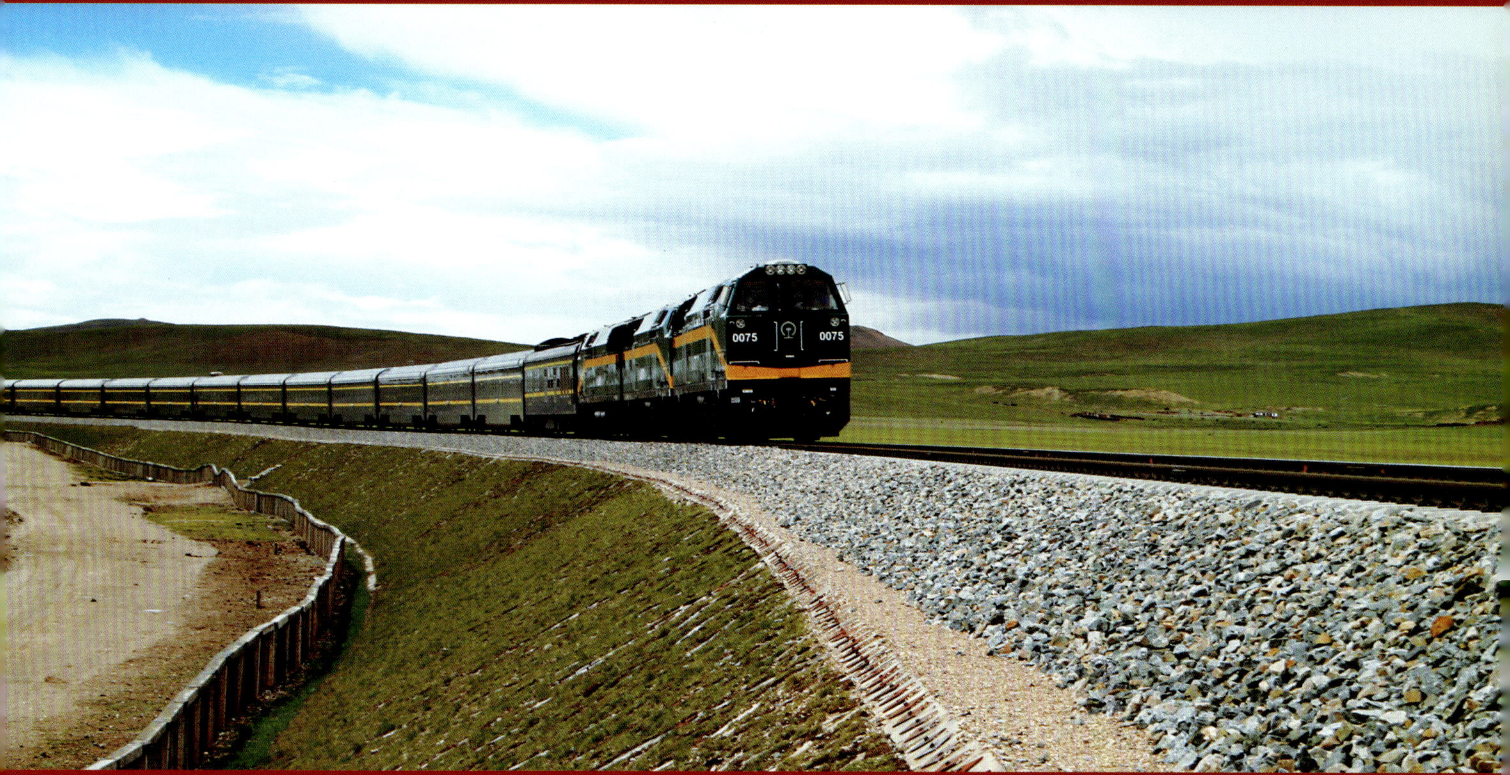

ENGINEERED SLOPES IN CHINA

–Approaches and Case Studies

中国典型工程边坡

◆◆◆◆◆◆◆

Highway and Railway Engineering Volume

交通工程卷

内 容 提 要

本卷画册从中国大量交通边坡工程中遴选出具有典型意义的公路和铁路边坡工程实例，描述了中国公路和铁路建设中跨越世界屋脊、高山峡谷、黄土沟壑、沙漠旱海、寒区冻土等特殊和极端恶劣环境条件地区的工程边坡问题，以及工程边坡建设的成功与失败事例，可供国内外广大土建工程研究、设计、施工等技术人员借鉴参考。

图书在版编目(CIP)数据

中国典型工程边坡. 交通工程卷 / 霍　明 ，王恭先主编.
北京：人民交通出版社，2008.6
ISBN　978-7-114-07206-2
Ⅰ.　中…　Ⅱ.①霍…②王…Ⅲ.①边坡－防护工程－中国
②交通工程－边坡－防护工程－中国　Ⅳ.U416.1
中国版本图书馆 CIP 数据核字(2008)第 080298 号

书　　名：中国典型工程边坡——交通工程卷
著 作 者：霍　明　王恭先
责任编辑：吴有铭　袁　方　曹延鹏
出版发行：人民交通出版社
地　　址：(100011)北京市朝阳区安定门外外馆斜街 3 号
网　　址：http://www.ccpress.com.cn
销售电话：(010)85285838，85285995
总 经 销：北京中交盛世书刊有限公司
经　　销：各地新华书店
印　　刷：北京华联印刷有限公司
开　　本：850 × 1230　1/16
印　　张：7
版　　次：2008 年 6 月第 1 版
印　　次：2008 年 6 月第 1 次印刷
书　　号：ISBN　978-7-114-07206-2
印　　数：0001-2000 册
定　　价：100.00 元

中国典型工程边坡

Engineered Slopes in China - Approaches and Case Studies

主　　编：陈祖煜　凤懋润

Editors-in-Chief: CHEN Zuyu　FENG Maorun

副 主 编：侯瑜京 王　园

Co-Editors-in-Chief: HOU Yujing　WANG Yuan

交通工程卷编写组

Editorial Board for the Highway and Railway Engineering Volume

主编单位：中交第一公路勘察设计研究院有限公司

参编单位：中铁西北科学研究院有限公司

Editored by: CCCC FIRST HIGHWAY CONSULTANTS CO., LTD.

NORTHWEST RESEARCH INSTITUTE CO., LTD. OF C.R.E.C

主　　编：霍　明　王恭先

Editors -in-Chief: HUO Ming　WANG Gongxian

执行主编：赵永国　贾志裕

Executive Editors-in-Chief:ZHAO Yongguo　JIA Zhiyu

副 主 编：赵永国　马惠民　王　园

Deputy Editors-in-Chief: ZHAO Yongguo　MA Huimin　WANG Yuan

编　　审：凤懋润　陈祖煜　喻文学　王传仁　谢永利　倪万魁　刘　涛

Professors of Editorship:FENG Maorun　CHEN Zuyu　YU Wenxue　WANG Chuanren　XIE Yongli　NI Wankui　LIU Tao

编　　写：喻林青　王学军　牛富俊　姜献民　焦　臣　罗满良　燕建民　路　勋　邓卫东　杨晓华
张建栋　蔡庆娥　李安洪　李　响　张　琼　石剑欣

Chief Editors: YU Linqing　WANG Xuejun　NIU Fujun　JIANG Xianmin　JIAO Chen　LUO Manliang　YAN Jianmin
LU Xun　DENG Weidong　YANG Xiaohua　ZHANG Jiandong　CAI Qing'e　LI Anhong　LI Xiang
ZHANG Qiong　SHI Jianxin

翻　　译：苏宝纨　吴宏伟　陈　锐　徐　洁　周公旦　蔡奇鹏　胡利文　江　娟　骆冠勇　周正兵　牛富俊　蔡庆娥

English Editors: So Po Yuen, Cynthia　Charles W.W.NG　CHEN Rui　XU Jie　ZHOU Gongdan　CAI Qipeng
HU Liwen　JIANG Juan　LUO Guanyong　ZHOU Zhengbing　NIU Fujun　CAI Qing'e

责任编辑：吴有铭　袁　方　曹延鹏

Editors in Charge: WU Youming　YUAN Fang　CAO Yanpeng

美术编辑：杨真朴

Art Editor: YANG Zhenpu

序 言

我国相当一部分国土处于崇山峻岭，遭受的滑坡和泥石流灾害十分严重。正在进行的大规模重大工程建设中的边坡稳定问题也至关重要。矿山、水利以及交通工程中发生的滑坡灾害带来了巨大的人员伤亡和财产损失。与此同时，三峡、小浪底以及青藏铁路等工程的成功建立也积累了大量的宝贵经验。

致力于减轻地质灾害和边坡工程研究的中国工程师和学者非常荣幸有机会主办2008年第10届国际滑坡与工程边坡会议。经讨论，我们决定出版有关中国滑坡和工程边坡的两个姐妹画册。中国典型滑坡画册由殷跃平博士主编，于2007年12月出版。中国典型工程边坡画册分别包括矿山工程卷、交通工程卷、水利水电工程卷及三峡库区卷。现在，我们非常高兴地看到，在各位同仁的共同努力下，该系列画册的出版已经成为现实。

本系列画册描述了工程建设中的一些重要的滑坡实例。盐池河滑坡和韩城电厂地面变形是由于地下开采引起的两个典型例子。前者掩埋了一个村庄，导致284人死亡；后者对边坡的变形和破坏影响持续了20年之久。由开挖引起的滑坡失事比较普遍。天生桥二级、小湾及漫湾等水电工程的教训值得我们重视。千将坪滑坡是三峡水库蓄水后的一次失事实例，尽管128人成功撤离，但仍导致了24人死亡。还有大量的位于黄土地区、寒冻土地区和沙漠地区的公路与铁路边坡，独具中国特色。

该画册还包括了若干成功的重大工程边坡实例。三峡船闸高边坡开挖石方量达$22 \times 10^6 m^3$，应力释放问题受到普遍关注，争论热烈，现在已经得到了答案。小浪底进、出口边坡位于第三纪砂岩与厚黏土夹层之上。在这个边坡布置了165m高土石坝的全部引水系统，施工期及运行期的成功运用，对这个黄河上的主要工程的安全极为重要。锦屏拱坝高达304m，开挖深度达530m，边坡坡度陡竣，达1：0.5～1：0.3。读者还会惊叹于那些描述三峡工程120万移民新城镇的图片。为了确保这些边坡的安全我们做了大量的工作。

我们真诚地感谢国务院三峡工程建设委员会办公室、中国水电工程顾问集团公司、中国矿业大学（北京）以及中交第一公路勘察设计研究院有限公司提供的经济资助以及在收集资料方面所做的努力；特别感谢那些提供宝贵图片和文档的人员，虽然不能在此一一列出他们的名字；特别感谢谭国焕教授、岳中琦教授、吴宏伟教授和殷建华教授，是他们组织人员进行了翻译；特别感谢苏宝纨女士，她和她的助手们志愿翻译了四卷画册的中文。没有他们的努力，该画册英文内容的出版几乎是不可能的。

陈祖煜
凤懋润

FOREWORD

With its large and mountainous topography, China has suffered from serious landslide and mudflow hazards. The large-scale economic construction has also raised serious slope stability concerns. Catastrophic landslides happened in the engineered slopes created in mining, hydropower and transportation projects, bringing huge losses of human lives and properties. On the other hand, valuable experiences have been obtained from many successful engineering slopes such as those involved in the projects of Three Gorges, Xiaolangdi, and the Qinghai-Tibet Railway, etc.

The Chinese engineers and scholars working on geohazard mitigations and slope engineering are particularly privileged to have the opportunity of hosting the 10th International Symposium on Landslides and Engineered Slopes in 2008. After a warm discussion, we decided to publish the sister-volumes of albums entitled 'Landslides in China - Selected Case Studies' and 'Engineered Slopes in China - Approaches and Case Studies' respectively as gifts to the Symposium. The landslide volume was edited by Dr. YIN Yueping and published in December, 2007. This 'early bird' brought great pressure and encouragement to us who had taken the responsibility of compiling the latter, an even big collection that consists of 4 volumes concerned with slopes of mining, highway and railway, water resources and hydropower, and the Three Gorges Reservoir projects respectively. We are happy to see that this album has now come to reality as a result of the joint efforts made by our colleagues working on different industrial and civil areas.

This album describes some important slope failure cases in engineering. The landslide of Yanchihe and the large ground movement of the Hancheng Power Plant are typical examples of slope failures induced by underground mining. The former buried a village and killed 284 people, and the latter caused more than 20 years sustaining slope movement and damages to the power plant. Landslides triggered by excavations are common and the slope failure cases of Tianshenqiao II, Xiaowan and Manwan projects are certainly worthwhile to be studied. Qianjianping Landslide is one case of slope failure caused by filling of the Three Gorge reservoir. Although 128 people had successfully evacuated, it still resulted in 24 fatalities.still many engineered slopes on highways and railways in the area of loess, frozen soil and deserst are specific in china.

This album contains a number of large-scale successful engineered slopes. The navigation lock of the Three Gorges project involves an excavation of 22×10^6 m^3 rocks and the issue of stress release had been a serious concern, to which the answer is available now. The intake and outlet slopes of the Xiaolangdi Project were built in Tertiary inter-bedded sandstones with thick clay seams. As these slopes accommodate all water diversion facilities of this 165 m high embankment dam, the successful performance during construction and operation has been a great contribution to this key project in the Yellow River. The left abutment of the 304 m high Jinping arch dam necessitates a 530 m deep excavation with a sloping of 0.5~0.3 (H) on 1 (V). Readers will also be impressed by the pictures that describe the new cities for the 1.2 million resettlement people of the Three Gorges Project. Tremendous efforts have been made to ensure safe performance of these slopes.

We would like to extend our sincere thanks to Office of Three Gorges Construction Council under the State Council, China Hydropower Engineering Consulting Group Corporation, China University of Mining & Technology ,Beijing and CCCC First Highway Consultants Co., Ltd for their financial support and efforts in collecting all the necessary information. Special thanks also go to those who offered their valuable photos and documents. To mention them one by one appears to be impossible, but their contributions will be remembered. We are particularly indebted to Professors George Tham, YUE Zhongqi, Charles Ng and YIN Jianhua from Hong Kong, who organized the English translation work. We are especially grateful to Mrs. So Po Yuen, Cynthia, who edited the English language voluntarily for all the 4 volumes based on her technical assistant's work. Without their effort, the English texts of this book would not have been made possible.

CHEN Zuyu
FENG Maorun

前　言

中国地域辽阔，地质条件十分复杂，地貌类型齐全，而且在独特的自然地理条件下，还发育了典型的黄土地貌、冻土地貌、风沙地貌等。在中国，山地、高原、丘陵面积约占国土面积的70%，由于山区地形地貌起伏多变，公路与铁路路基的修筑就不可避免地要出现填、挖，从而形成众多的工程边坡。同时由于山区地质条件复杂，地质环境脆弱，地质灾害发育，道路工程建设中不合理的切坡、填沟等工程活动必然会对地质环境造成破坏，还会诱发和加剧各种地质灾害，从而酿成各种类型的边坡病害。

20世纪50年代以来，伴随着中国经济的快速发展，铁路与公路建设逐步向山区延伸，工程边坡的数量和规模迅速增加，由边坡引起的工程与环境问题也日益突出。尤其是20世纪90年代中后期，我国山区高速公路建设飞速发展，公路建设中的高边坡工程数量之多、规模之大、类型之复杂、工程之艰巨，举世瞩目。

为向世人展示中国在公路与铁路工程边坡建设方面取得的业绩，总结工程边坡治理的经验与教训，借第10届国际滑坡与工程边坡会议在中国召开之际，编写组从中国大量的边坡工程实例和相关资料中，遴选出有一定典型意义的公路与铁路边坡工程，汇编为《中国典型工程边坡（交通工程卷）》。

本画册共分三大单元：第一单元（第1章）回顾评价了中国公路与铁路边坡工程的历史与现状；第二单元（第2章）详细展示了中国山区公路与铁路建设中的若干典型边坡案例；第三单元（第3、4、5章）分别展示了独具中国特色的黄土地区、寒冻地区、沙漠地区的公路与铁路边坡工程。

本画册由中交第一公路勘察设计研究院有限公司中交寒区道路工程重点实验室开放基金资助出版，由中交第一公路勘察设计研究院有限公司和中铁西北科学研究院具体组织编写，由喻文学、王传仁、谢永利三位专家主审。赵永国教授级高工为本画册的成书做了大量艰苦细致的调研和编辑工作。

本画册在编写过程中承蒙众多单位及相关人员提供资料。画册中还引用了国内外许多学者的研究成果和资料。在此对所有支持本书出版的专家和同志表示衷心感谢！

编写组

2007年8月18日

PREFACE

China is a vast country with complicated geological conditions and complex geomorphology. Typical landforms of loess, frozen soil and wind-borne sand are developed under its special physiographic conditions. In China, mountain regions, plateaus and hills cover a total of 70% of the whole country area. In the mountain regions, extensions of roads and railways both in terms of scale and numbers are inevitable. Then many engineering slopes occur. For the reasons of the complicated geological conditions, the weak geological environment and developed geological hazards in mountain regions, some engineering activities in road constructions, such as unreasonable slope cutting and gully filling, will destroy geological environment and induce or intensify all kinds of geological hazards. They will cause different types of slope failures.

Since the 1950s, with the rapid development of Chinese economy, highway and railway construction has gradually extended to the mountainous regions. At the same time, the number and scale of engineered slopes have surged, bringing into prominence the engineering and environmental problems caused by such slopes. The late 1990s saw the peak of such developments when the construction of expressways in the mountainous regions made a quantum leap. The number, scale, complexity in types and difficulty of construction of the high slopes involved in road construction caught worldwide attention.

In order to share China's experience and achievements in highway and railway engineered slope construction with the world, the editorial committee has selected typical cases of highway and railway engineered slopes, and compiled Book of Engineered Slopes in China (Highway and Railway Engineering Volume) to coincide with the 10th International Symposium on Landslide and Engineered Slopes to be held in June 2008, China.

This book consists of three parts. In part one (Chapter 1), the development of highway and railway slope engineering in China is reviewed and evaluated. In part two (Chapter 2), typical cases of engineered slopes in the construction of highways and railways in mountainous areas are illustrated. In part three (Chapters 3, 4 and 5), engineered slopes on highways and railways in the unique loess, frozen soil, and desert regions in China are shown respectively.

The book was sponsored by an open fund from the Key Laboratory on Road Engineering in Frozen Soil Regions, First Highway Consultant Co., Ltd (FHCC). It was organized and compiled by FHCC and Northwest Research Institute Co., Ltd. of China Railway Engineering Corporation. The book was checked by YU Wenxue, WANG Chuanren, XIE Yongli. Professor ZHAO Yongguo worked hard and made considerable contribution to this book in research and editing.

It is grateful to the units and individuals who provided relevant information during the compilation of this book. The book has also cited research results and data of researchers at home and abroad. We would like to express our gratitude to all the experts who have made this publication possible.

Editorial Committee

18 August 2007

目 录

CONTENTS

第Ⅰ章　中国公路与铁路工程边坡的历史与现状 …… (1)
Chapter I Development of Highway & Railway Engineered Slopes (1)

第Ⅱ章　中国山区公路与铁路建设中的典型工程边坡 …… (21)
Chapter II Highway & Railway Engineered Slopes in Mountainous Areas (21)

第Ⅲ章　中国黄土高原地区的公路工程边坡 …… (57)
Chapter III Highway Engineered Slopes in Loess Plateau Regions (57)

第Ⅳ章　中国寒区的公路与铁路工程边坡 …… (71)
Chapter IV Highway & Railway Engineered Slopes in Frozen Ground Regions (71)

第Ⅴ章　中国沙漠地区的公路与铁路工程边坡 …… (83)
Chapter V Highway & Railway Engineered Slopes in Desert Areas (83)

附　录　中国公路与铁路工程边坡技术创新的代表性机构 …… (97)
APPENDIX Representative Institution for Technological Innovation on Highway & Railway Engineered Slopes (97)

第Ⅰ章　中国公路与铁路工程边坡的历史与现状

Chapter I Development of Highway & Railway Engineered Slopes

公路和铁路都是具有一定空间几何标准的线状工程，受山区地质、地貌条件的限制和公路、铁路几何标准的制约，山区筑路不可避免地要切割山体或对既有边坡灾害进行整治，从而形成大量的工程边坡。20世纪50年代以来，伴随着中国经济的快速发展、丘陵和山区的开发利用、铁路与公路向山区延伸，边坡稳定问题变得日益突出，相应地其理论研究和防治工程技术也得到迅速发展。其发展演变具有以下几个特点：

（1）在建设规模上，经历了由少到多、单体规模由小到大的迅速扩张，并形成两个高峰期：一个是20世纪50～60年代以宝成铁路、川藏公路等为代表的一大批山区公路、铁路建设形成的工程边坡；另一个是20世纪90年代以来，大量山区高速公路建设所形成的工程边坡。

（2）在治理理念上，经历了由“先破坏后治理”→“一次根治、不留后患”→“预防为主、综合治理”的转变，人地关系日趋和谐。

（3）在防护加固形式上，经历了由“少防护或无防护”→“以高大圬工混凝土或浆砌工程防护为主”→“刚柔结构相结合、多层防护与生态植被防护相结合”的演变，防护体系日趋完善。

（4）特殊复杂高边坡的勘察设计和监测、测试技术日益成熟。主要表现是普遍重视了针对高边坡的工程地质勘察工作，基于综合监测、测试获取的信息进行“动态设计、信息化施工”。

Highway and railway structures are linear constructions with spatial and geometrical specifications. Due to geological topographical and road geometry constraints, road construction in mountainous areas requires slope cutting or treatment of existing failed slopes, giving rise to a large number of engineered slopes along the highway. With the rapid development of the Chinese economy since the 1950s, hilly and mountainous areas have been developed and railways and highways have been extending into these regions. This highlighted the issue of slope stability and gave impetus to relevant theoretical research and prevention and control technology. Several characteristics of development are presented as follows.

(1) In terms of scale of construction, it has gone from less to more, and from single entities to rapid expansion, culminating in two peak periods. The first period was from 1950s to 1960s, when a large number of engineered slopes came into being as a result of highway construction in mountainous areas, representative projects being the Baoji-Chengdu Railway and the Sichuan-Tibet Highway. The second period was from the 1990s onwards, when the construction of expressways in mountainous areas gave rise to large numbers of engineered slopes.

(2) With regard to treatment approach, it has evolved first from “damage followed by treatment” into “radical treatment once and for all”, and then into “protection and comprehensive treatment”, which makes for a more harmonic relationship between man and land.

(3) In terms of protection measures, they have gone from “little or no protection” to “mainly massive concrete or mortared rubble masonry structures”, and “more recently to a combination of rigid and flexible structures by using multi-layered protection and vegetation”. Protection systems are being perfected all the time.

(4) Survey design, monitoring and testing techniques for special and complex high slopes are becoming more sophisticated each day. It is shown in the general emphasis placed on the geological investigation of these slopes, and the implementation of “dynamic design and informed construction” based on information obtained from comprehensive monitoring and testing.

■20世纪50年代，国家物流急需铁路大干快上，宝（鸡）成（都）铁路、陇海铁路宝鸡至天水段、鹰（潭）厦（门）铁路等山区铁路相继开工建设，经验不足、技术薄弱等导致在铁路建设中发生众多边坡失稳变形和古滑坡复活，影响久远。如宝成铁路全长669km，沿线共发生比较严重的边坡病害447处，个别高边坡病害历经30多年才得到根治。

■In the 1950s, in order to meet national logistic requirements, there was large-scale and rapid construction of railways such as the Baoji-Chengdu Railway, the Long-Hai Railway extension from Baoji to Tianshui, and the Yingtan-Xiamen Railway. Due to inadequate experience and poor techniques available that time, road construction led to instability and deformation of many slopes and the revival of fossil landslides. This remained problematic for a long time. For instance, the Bao-Cheng Railway, with a total length of 669km, experienced 447 slope failures. Some high slope failures were only resolved after more than 30 years.

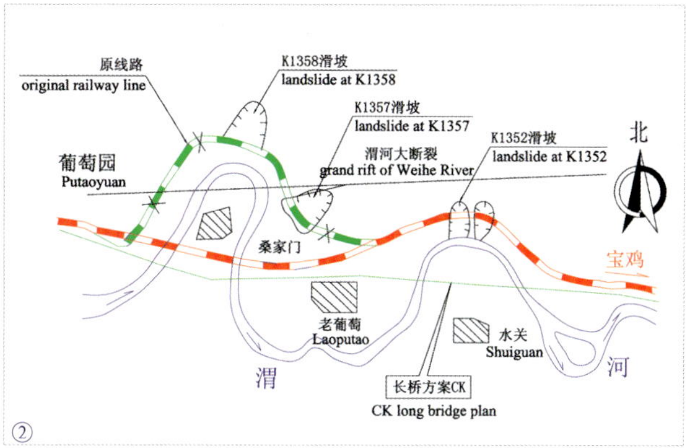

图1.1　陇海铁路宝鸡至天水段被誉为中国铁路的“盲肠”。1963年发生K1358滑坡(左)，1981年发生的K1357高速远程滑坡(右)使渭河断流。为彻底避开滑坡危害，不得不两跨渭河改移线路。

Fig 1.1 The Long-Hai Railway extension from Baoji to Tianshui is named the "caecum" of Chinese railway. A slide took place in 1963 at milestone K1358 (left side in the figure). A high-speed landslide (right side) in 1981 had a far runout distance and blocked the Weihe River. To avoid further slides, two railway bridges were built across the Weihe River as a diversion.

■ 20世纪50～70年代，川藏公路、新藏公路、天山公路等国家干线公路相继建设，受当时经济条件的制约，公路路线平纵指标较低，路基填挖规模一般较小，公路沿线的边坡以自然坡面为主，边坡基本不做防护，主要靠后期养护、抢修维持通行，公路抗灾能力较差，许多路段或因地质灾害多发，或因人工开挖（填筑）破坏而留下诸多边坡隐患。

■ From the 1950s to 1970s, the Sichuan-Tibet Highway, Xinjiang-Tibet Highway and Tianshan Highway were constructed successively. Due to economic constraints, the alignment standard of the highways was low, and road base excavations were generally small-scale. The slopes along the highways were primarily natural slopes with little protection, relying mainly on subsequent maintenance and repair to keep the roads clear, and were more failure prone. As a result, many road segments became problematic due to frequent geological disasters, or damage by excavation (cut and fill).

新藏公路K149段

K149 section in Xinjiang-Tibet highway

图1.2　穿行于西昆仑山区峡谷地带的新藏公路，常因边破坍塌、坠石及路基水毁而断道。(童海刚　摄)

Fig 1.2 A section of the Xinjiang-Tibet Highway through the west Kunlun valley is often blocked by slope collapse, rock fall and pavement erosion. (TONG Haigang)

川藏公路大柏牛崩塌 *Daboniu rock avalanche in Sichuan-Tibet highway*

图1.3 川藏公路前龙段在修建和改造过程中，以切坡方式通过岩性破碎、构造复杂的区域，引发了大规模的边坡病害群。（王传仁 摄）

Fig 1.3 The Sichuan-Tibet Highway passed through a slope composed of crushed rocks in the Qianlong section. Large-scale landslides were induced .(WANG Chuanren)

■ 20世纪60年代以来，中国铁路建设认真汲取了宝成线等山区铁路建设中的经验和教训，采取了“预防为主”的原则，在选线阶段采用较多的隧道和桥梁方案而避免了大量的高边坡工程，并总结提出了“治早治小”、“一次根治、不留后患”的经验，出现了以抗滑桩、锚杆挡墙为代表的新型支挡结构以及桩墙结合、桩隧结合、桩板结合的边坡病害治理结构。

■ Since the 1960s, based upon the experience gained in the construction of the Baoji-Chengdu Railway in the mountainous areas, railway construction in China has adopted the principle of “prevention over cure”, giving preference to schemes comprising more tunnels and bridges at the route planning stage to avoid too many high-rising slopes. With the adoption of the principles of “A stitch in time saves nine” and “radical treatment once and for all”, various structures have been used to protect slopes: new support structures such as slope stabilizing piles and anchored retaining walls, and comprehensive protection measures such as piles combined with retaining walls, piles combined with tunnels and pile combined with plates.

图1.4 襄（樊）渝（重庆）铁路赵家塘滑坡为巨型深层基岩滑坡。采取抗滑桩和抗滑挡土墙整治，抗滑桩最大截面为4.5m × 7.5m，最大桩长47m。

Fig 1.4 A large-scale landslide took place at Zhaojiatang, Xiang-Yu Railway, which was a typical deep slide in the bedrock. Slope stabilizing piles and Antiskid retaining walls were used to repair the slope. The piles have a maximum cross section of 4.5 m × 7.5 m, and a maximum length of 47 m.

图1.5　西安至南京铁路岭底滑坡为一处于不稳定状态的巨型老滑坡。采取桩板复合结构整治，抗滑桩截面 3.5m × 3.5m，桩长 21 ~ 30m，桩间设置挡土板。

Fig 1.5　A massive fossil landslide took place on an unstable slope at Lindi, Xi'an-Nanjing Railway. The slope was repaired by a combination of piles and plates. Thc slope stabilizing piles have a cross section of 3.5 m × 3.5 m, and a length of about 21~30 m. Retaining plates were installed between the piles.

图1.6　渝(重庆)怀(化)铁路武隆纸厂滑坡为一巨型堆积层滑坡。铁路采用隧道穿越滑坡中部。采用抗滑桩、抗冲刷挡土墙及河岸防护工程综合整治滑坡。

Fig 1.6　A huge scale deposit landslide took place near Wulong Paper Workshop, Yu-Huai Railway. A tunnel was cut through thc middle part of the landslide, and comprehensive measures were taken to protect the slope, namely slope stabilizing pile, erosion resistant retaining walls and embankment protection buildings.

■20世纪90年代以来，中国高速公路建设迅猛发展并逐步向山区延伸，其标准高、路幅宽，尽管有的路段桥隧比例已占路线的30%以上，但仍在工程建设中形成了大量的高陡边坡。而这些高边坡当中稳定性差和不稳定的高边坡占了较大比例。高速公路高边坡问题在20世纪中后期成为一个非常具有中国特色的重大工程地质问题。

■Since the 1990s, the construction of expressways in China has progressed at great speed and has gradually extended to mountainous areas. The construction standards are high and the road surfaces are wide. Although bridges and tunnels already account for over 30% in certain road sections, many high slopes have nevertheless been formed. Among these slopes, most are unstable. The highway slope problem had become a major geological engineering issue for China by the latter half of the 20th century.

图1.7　某山区高速公路路堑高边坡在施工中发生滑坡，已施工的防护工程遭到破坏。

Fig 1.7　A landslide on expressway during construction, damaging protection structures already in place.

■传统的边坡的防护多以工程防护措施为主，且多采用混凝土或浆砌高挡墙、护坡、护面墙以及喷浆(混凝土)、锚杆挂网喷浆(混凝土)等进行大段落防护，边坡人工痕迹明显，与周围环境的协调性差。

■ Conventional slope protection often turns to engineering protection measures. In most cases, concreted or mortared retaining walls, slope covers, face wall covers and grouting, or shotcrete and anchors are used in large stretches, resulting in an obtrusively artificial look not in harmony with its surroundings.

图1.8　高大的浆砌片石护坡工程尤显突兀，与周围环境极不协调。(王园　摄)

Fig 1.8　This high-rising mortar rubble masonry work for slope protection appears particularly obtrusive against the backdrop of its surroundings. (WANG Yuan)

图1.9　高大、突显的路侧桩、墙支挡结构显得厚重、压抑。(朱聪功　摄)

Fig 1.9　This large and obtrusive roadside pile and retaining structure look massive and oppressive. (ZHU Conggong)

① 与周围绿色环境极不协调 *Incompatible with the green surroundings*

② 局部剥落 *Localized collapse*

图 1.10 20世纪90年代中后期曾一度流行的喷浆（混凝土）、锚杆挂网喷浆（混凝土）防护对环境破坏较大，不仅使坡面缺乏生机，且易开裂、剥落，耐久性差。（焦臣 摄）

Fig 1.10 Shotcrete and anchor and shotcrete protection popular during the mid to late 1990s have caused relatively more damage to the environment. Slopes surfaces lack life, easy to crack and peel,are of poor durability. (JIAO Chen)

■20世纪后期以来，中国交通行业将如何有效预防边坡失稳和造成灾害作为重要研究课题广泛深入地开展了研究，取得了显著成效，主要表现在：公路建设中普遍贯彻“地质选线”原则，绕避严重地质不良路段；强化对高边坡的综合工程地质勘察与评价，对潜在不稳定边坡采取“预加固”措施；控制路基填挖高度，尽可能地减少高边坡数量，降低边坡高度；边坡防护注重工程防护与生态植被防护相结合。

■Ever since the late 20th century, communication construction industries in China have carried out extensive and rigorous research on the prevention of slope instability and slope disasters with outstanding results. The achievements include upholding the principle of "geological considerations" in the choice of routes, avoiding imperfect geologic sections. Secondly, integrated geotechnical investigation and assessment of slopes are being enhanced, applying "proactive reinforcement" to potentially unstable slopes. Thirdly, the height of excavation of road bases is being controlled, the number of high slopes and the height of slopes are being reduced. Lastly, the integration of engineering protection and vegetation slope protection is favoured.

图1.11　青海马场垣至西宁高速公路利用竖向分离式路基、半桥半路及顺河纵向桥避免了因深挖而破坏原已稳定的天然边坡。（韩文宪　摄）

Fig 1.11　Vertical separated roadbeds, and a road-bridge generally parallel to the river were exploited to avoid failure of stable natural slopes by deep cutting on the expressway from Machangyuan, Qinghai to Xining. (HAN Wenxian)

图1.12　重庆渝黔高速公路采用半隧半路绕避边坡病害。（邓卫东　摄）

Fig 1.12　Tunnel-roads were used to avoid slope problems on the Express way from Chongqing to Guizhou. (DENG Weidong)

■植被防护不仅可防止边坡冲蚀破坏，而且还可以绿化环境，营造景观，近几年来日益受到中国公路与铁路建设的推崇。常采用的有：液力喷播绿化防护、三维网喷播绿化防护、挖沟（穴）绿化防护、客土喷播绿化防护、植被混凝土绿化防护、土工格室绿化防护等。

■Not only can vegetation protect slopes from erosion failure, but it can also help build a green environment and enhance the scenery. Vegetation slopes have been extensively used in highways and railways in China. Common methods used include hydraulic grouting vegetable seeds, shotcrete with 3D geonets, vegetation protection by digging trenches, vegetation protection by soil shotcrete or by concrete, and geogrid protection method, etc.

① 坡面挂网、喷射基材混合物

Geonets are used on slope surface and mixture of seeds and soil is shotcreted

② 无纺布养生、植物发芽

Vegetation on slope is formed

③ 坡面植被形成

Seedling comes out from slope surface

④ 坡面植物长成幼苗

Nonwoven fabric assists seeds to burgeon

图1.13 客土喷播绿化防护。信阳至南阳高速公路沿坡面锚挂14号镀锌铁丝网，网孔5cm × 5cm，锚钉间距1.5m，长40～80cm；基材混合物按不同配比分两次喷播，其中基层厚度8cm，面层厚1cm。（石剑欣　提供）

Fig 1.13 Vegetation protection by shotcrete with soils. No.14 Zincified steel nets were anchored on the slope surface, with 50 mm ×50 mm openings, nails spacings of 1.5 m and nail lengths of 400 mm to 800 mm. Mixture of seeds with soil was shotcreted twice in different composition ratios. The thickness of the base is 80 mm and that of the face cover is 10 mm on the Expressway from Xinyang to Nanyang. (SHI Jianxin)

图1.14　轮胎固土绿化技术。宁杭高速公路用废旧轮胎在岩石坡面上固土护坡，建立草灌复合植被。

Fig 1.14　Vegetation technique using tyres to reinforce soils. Rock slopes are stabilized by abandoned tyres. Vegetation with a mixture of grass and shrub is established on the Ningbo-Hangzhou Expressway.

图1.15　草棍客土喷播。宁杭高速公路在岩石风化较为严重的路段，用稻草缠绕毛竹杆成草棍，经稀泥浸泡、固定并喷上营养土，在其上喷播并栽植美人蕉、扶芳藤等多种植物。

Fig 1.15　Soils are shotcreted on grass sticks. This method is used on seriously weathered rock slopes. Bamboo sticks are first wrapped in straw, and then immersed in slurry. Nutrimental soil is then grouted on the sticks. Finally, canna and liana are planted on the slopes on the Ningbo-Hangzhou Expressway.

■植被防护与工程防护结合，可达到加固与防护兼顾、刚柔相济的效果。目前在路基边坡防护中广泛采用的有：浆砌片石骨架或混凝土骨架植被防护、多边形混凝土空心砖植被防护、锚杆（锚索）混凝土框架植被防护等。骨架可以采用拱形、窗孔形、人字形、菱形、矩形等多种形式。

■ The combined approach of using vegetation together with engineering structures for slope protection achieves consolidating as well as protection effects. Currently, popular protection methods using vegetation for roadbed slopes are rubble masonry or concrete aggregate, polygon hollow concrete bricks, anchored concrete frame. Supporting frames can be made in an arch shape, window-hole shape, " ^ " shape, diamond shape and rectangular shape, etc.

图1.16　京珠高速粤境北段采用浆砌片石方格骨架植被防护路堑边坡。(王园　摄)

Fig 1.16　Rubble masonry slopes with vegetation were used in cut slopes at North Canton section on the Beijing-Zhuhai Expressway. (WANG Yuan)

图1.17　贵州镇宁至黄果树高速公路采用浆砌片石方格骨架(排水式)植被防护填方高边坡。(赵刚　摄)

Fig 1.17　Rubble masonry grid frame (drainage type) with vegetation protection was adopted in fill slope on the expressway from Zhenning to Huangguoshu in Guizhou Province. (ZHAO Gang)

图1.18 广东汕头至梅州高速公路预应力锚索框架与植被防护结合。(邓卫东 提供)

Fig 1.18 Prestressed anchor frame with vegetation was used to protect slopes on the Shantou-Meizhou expressway, Guangdong. (DENG Weidong)

图1.19 广西桂林至南宁高速公路采用水泥混凝土"人"字形骨架植被防护的路堑边坡。(王园 摄)

Fig 1.19 "^" shaped concrete frame was used with vegetation to protect cut slopes on the Guilin-Nanning expressway, Guangxi. (WANG Yuan)

图1.20　川主寺至九寨沟公路采用阶梯式护面墙结合绿化防护的路堑边坡。(张永刚　提供)

Fig 1.20 Stepwise retaining walls were used with vegetation to prevent failure of cut slopes on the Chuanzhusi-Jiuzhaigou Highway.(ZHANG Yonggang)

■柔性防护系统越来越多地应用于公路与铁路边坡的防护，不仅可有效防止边坡的局部崩塌碎落，而且有利于边坡的自然恢复。

■ Flexible protection systems have increasingly been adopted in highway and railway slope engineering. Not only can localized collapse of slopes be effectively prevented, but also the ecology of slopes can be rehabilitated naturally.

①

图1.21　内(江)昆(明)铁路主动与被动防护网防护。

Fig 1.21 Passive protection wire net was used for the Neijiang-Kunming Railway.

图1.22　万(州)开(县)高速公路主动防护网防护。

Fig 1.22 Active protection wire net was used for the Wangzhou-Kaixian Expressway.

图1.23　国道214线采用石笼挡墙防护。（赵永国　摄）

Fig 1.23　Stone cage retaining walls were used to protect slopes on the No.214 national highway. (ZHAO Yongguo)

■滑坡和高边坡病害加固处治技术方面，在继承一系列适应不同地质条件的传统抗滑支挡结构形式的基础上，边坡加固尤其是岩石高边坡加固普遍采用预应力锚索（杆）锚固技术，主要有锚索抗滑桩、锚墩、锚索地梁、锚索（杆）框架、锚索挡墙（肋板墙）、土钉墙等结构形式。微型桩和各种注浆加固技术等也普遍应用。

■ With regard to protection techniques for treating landslides and slope disasters, prestressed anchors have been extensively adopted to reinforce slopes, based on previous experience with different retaining walls. There are many measures available, such as anchor reinforced piles, anchorages, anchored earth beams, anchored frames, anchored retaining walls and soil nails. Different types of mini-piles and grouting have also been adopted.

①　悬臂式钢筋混凝土抗滑桩

Cantilever reinforced concrete slope stabilizing pile

②　预应力锚索抗滑桩

Slope stabilizing pile with prestressed cables

③　桩间设护面墙的抗滑桩

Face cover used between slope stabilizing piles

④　桩间设挡土板的抗滑桩

Retaining plates used between slope stabilizing piles

图1.24　抗滑桩是治理大中型滑坡最主要的支挡工程结构。抗滑桩常与预应力锚索、钢筋混凝土挡板、桩间护面墙等组成复合结构，大量使用在边坡的坡脚加固工程中。

Fig 1.24　Slope stabilizing piles are mainly used to treat medium to large-scale landslides. Slope stabilizing piles are applied with prestressed anchor bars, reinforced retaining plates, protection face covers as a composite structure, to reinforce the slope toes.

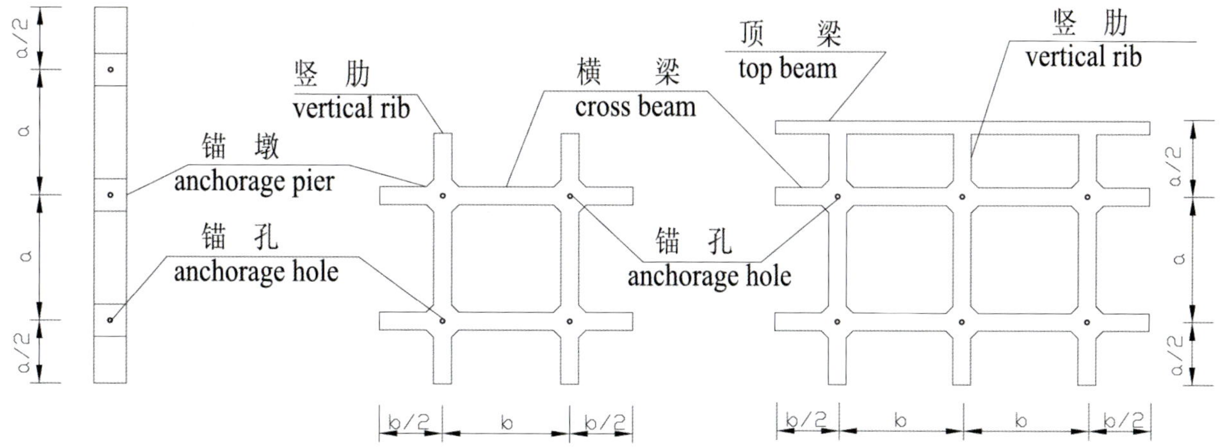

① 应力锚索地梁、锚索框架梁示意图
Sketch map of the foundation beam & frame beam with prestressed cables

② 锚墩群
Anchorage piers

③ 锚索地梁
Foundation beam with prestressed cables

④ 锚索框架梁
Frame beam with cables (No.1)

⑤ 锚索框架梁
Frame beam with cables (No.2)

图 1.25 预应力锚索体系由预应力锚索和墩、梁、框架等共同构成，具有结构简单、施工安全、对坡体扰动小、可迅速起到稳定坡体或减缓坡体变形等诸多优点，近年来在铁路、公路建设中发展迅速，使用广泛。

Fig 1.25 The prestressed cable structure system is composed of prestressed cable and pier, beam or frame. The system is easy to construct and causes little disturbance. It can stabilize the slope or decrease the slope deformation quickly, and hence has been widely used for highways and railways recently.

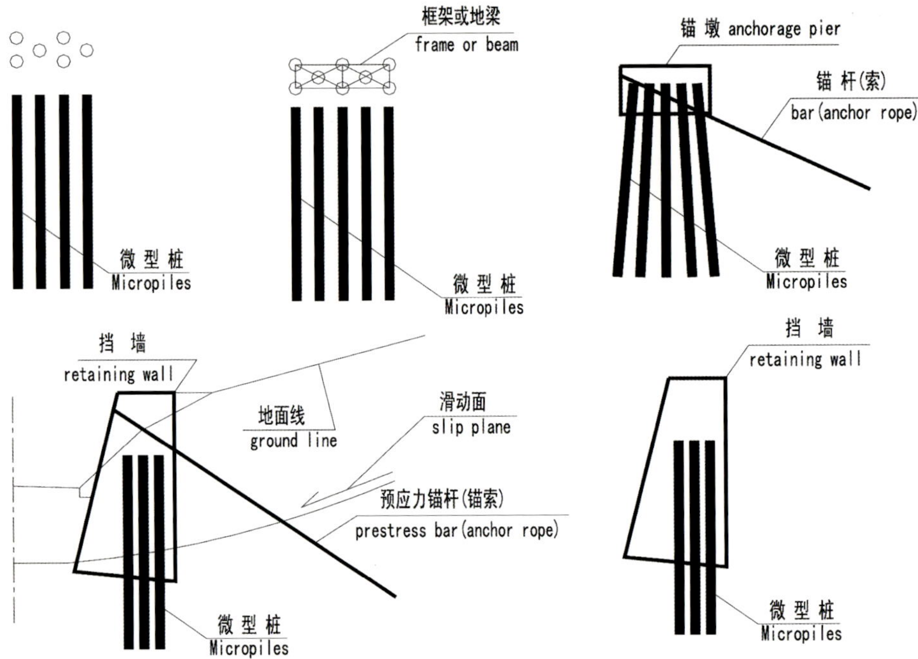

图1.26 微型桩是近年来用于高边坡加固工程的新型加固工程结构，具有快速、方便、灵活的优点，目前已在国道317线等多项公路边坡加固工程中得到了成功应用。微型桩与框架梁或墩、锚索（杆）、挡墙等组合可形成不同的结构形式。

Fig 1.26 The mini-pile has been applied to reinforce high slopes recently. Its advantages are short construction time, ease of construction and location flexibility. Many high slopes in national highway No.317 have been successfully reinforced by mini-piles. Different composite structures can be formed by combining mini-piles with frame beams, piers, anchors or retaining walls.

■近年来基于“强腰固脚”的原理，在实践中逐步探索出了一套边坡加固工程的组合结构类型。如“桩－锚”结构、“墙－锚”结构、“桩－桩”结构和“减重－锚(桩)”结构，这些组合结构特别适合于高大、复杂边坡的治理工程。

■ *Based on the principle of "protection of slope waist and reinforcement of slope toe", composite structures have been invented to prevent high and problematic slopes from sliding. They are the pile-anchor structure, retaining wall-anchor structure, pile-pile structure, load reduction-anchor pile structure.*

图1.27　京珠高速粤境北段K108滑坡为富水型破碎煤系地层与松散残坡积层滑坡，滑坡区有四条断层密集分布。由于对其复杂性认识不足，治理方案反复5次后才得以根治。滑坡治理采取了刷方减载、抗滑桩、截排水盲洞、微型钢管压力灌注桩、锚杆框架等多种措施，框架内采用植草或六棱砖植草护坡防护。整治后的工程边坡共分八级，每级坡高6m，坡率1∶1，最高48m。(王恭先　提供)

Fig 1.27　A landslide, located at section K108 of the Beijing-Zhuhai expressway, was triggered in a fractured stratum and loose deposit with a high water content. Four faults are distributed closely in the area. Treatment succeeded finally after 5 trials. Many measures were used to treat the landslide combined with the vegetation slope method, such as unloading by digging the slope, slope stabilizing pile, blind drainage hole, mini-steel bored pile, anchored frame, and so on. The whole slope, whose maximum height was 48 m, contained 8 levels, each 6m high at a slope ratio of 1:1. (WANG Gongxian)

①　施工中的锚索框架梁

Frame beam with cables under construction

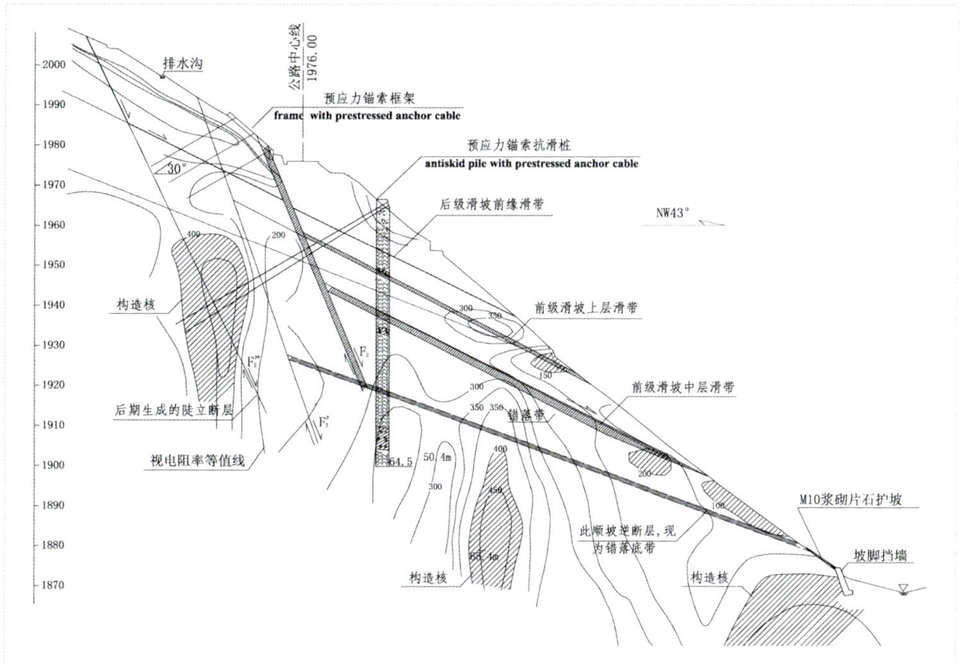

②　1号滑坡整治工程典型断面图

Typical cross-section of No.1 Landslide treatment project

图1.28　川藏公路前龙滑坡群1号滑坡是一处具有多级、多条、多滑带等特点的大型复杂滑坡。治理采用了预应力锚索框架、普通抗滑桩、预应力锚索抗滑桩等结构。实际实施的锚索长度达到了73m，抗滑桩长度达到了67m，整治效果良好。(马惠民　提供)

Fig 1.28　No.1 landslide in the Sichuan-Tibet highway was a large-scale and complicated landslide with multiple levels, multiple strips and potential sliding zones. The treatment measures included prestressed anchor frames, conventional slope stabilizing piles and prestressed cable slope stabilizing pile structures. The length of anchor cables was 73 m and the length of slope stabilizing piles was 67 m. The treatment worked well. (MA Huimin)

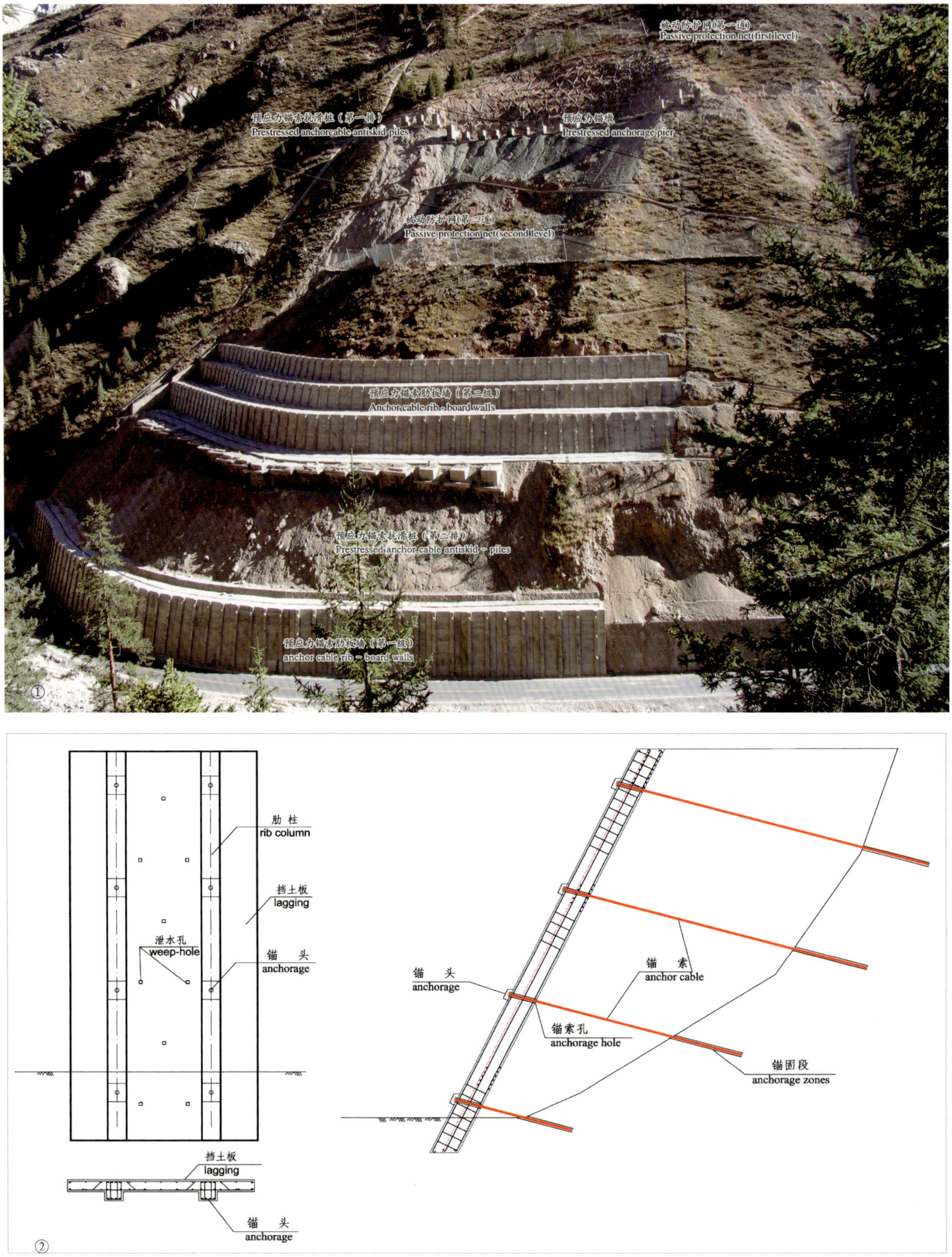

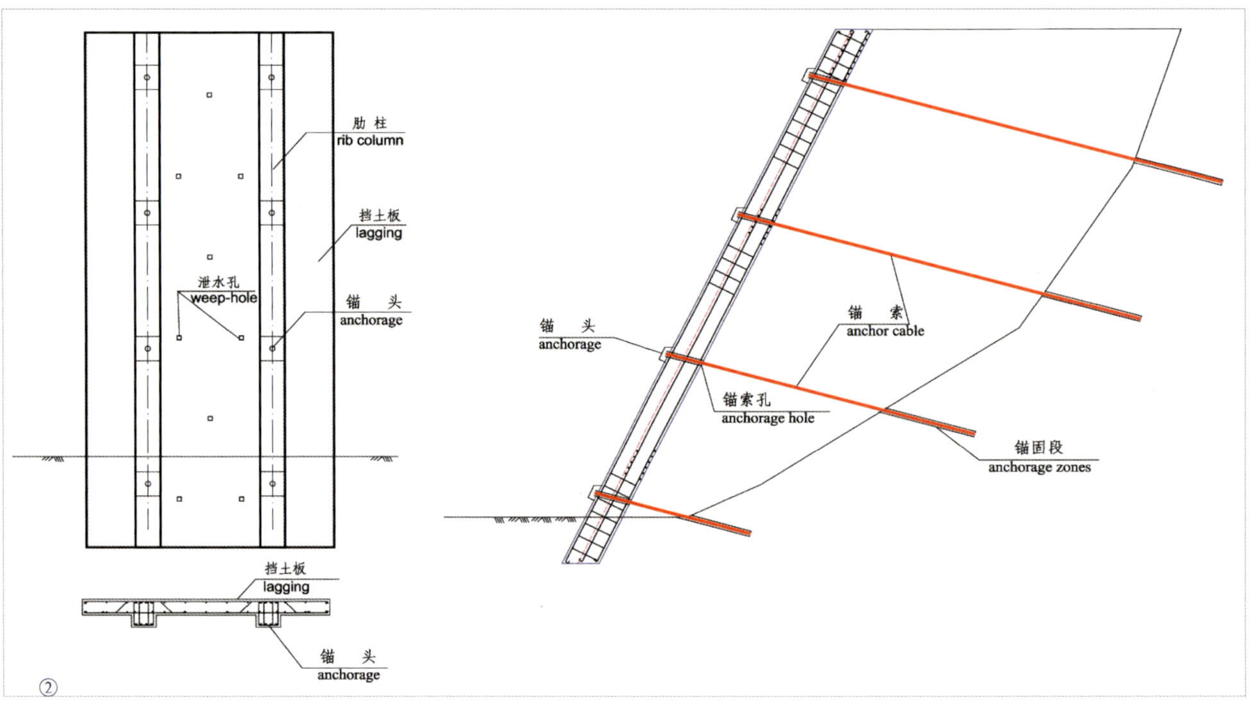

图 1.29 国道 317 线安坝至昌都公路 K369 滑坡采用预应力锚索肋板挡墙（2 级）和预应力锚索抗滑桩（2 排）、锚墩、被动防护网（2 道）等组成的“桩 - 锚 - 墙 - 网”组合结构综合治理高大边坡。（路勋 提供）

Fig 1.29 A complex pil-anchor-wall-net structure was adopted to treat the high slope in section K369 of No.317 national highway. In the protection system, two levels of prestressed cable rib-board walls, two rows of prestressed cable slope stabilizing piles, anchorage piers and two rows of passive protection nets were combined to repair the slope. (LU Xun)

■水是影响边坡稳定和诱发边坡变形失稳最主要的因素之一，因此加强边坡区的地表和地下排水已形成一种理念。地表排水工程主要有截水沟、排水沟和自然沟防渗，地下排水工程主要有支撑盲沟、截排水盲洞、垂直钻孔群排水、仰斜孔群排水、集水井群排水等。工程实践表明，这些适用于不同条件的截排水措施，在滑坡治理和边坡加固中是至关重要的。

■Pore water plays a key role in slope stability and in causing slope failure. Hence the enhancement of surface and mole drainage systems in slope areas has become a guiding principle. Surface drainage consists mainly of open catch drains, trenches and natural trenches to avoid seepage from top to toe. Mole drainage consists mainly of blind mole drains, vertical drain groups, inclined drain groups and collector well systems. It has been shown through engineering practice that drainage systems play an important role in treating landslides and reinforcing slopes.

图1.30 贵州镇宁至黄果树高速公路截水沟与排水沟。(赵刚 摄)

Fig 1.30 Open catch drain and trench on the Zhenning-Huangguoshu Expressway. (ZHAO Gang)

图1.31 铜川至黄陵高速公路仰斜孔群排水。(赵永国 摄)

Fig 1.31 Inclined drain group on the Tongchuan-Huangling Expressway. (ZHAO Yongguo)

■对于膨胀土路堑边坡防护，一般采用的全封闭式的圬工满铺防护方案治理膨胀土效果较差。信（阳）南（阳）高速公路、郑（州）石（人山）高速公路、襄（樊）渝（重庆）铁路复线等项目采用膨胀土生态改性剂处治膨胀土路堑边坡，取得了良好的技术经济效果。(陈永烽、石剑欣、李高旺 提供)

■The commonly adopted masonry method is not suitable for expansive soil cut slopes. Montmorillonite's Absorbent was adopted to treat cut slopes of expansive soil along the Xinyang-Nanyang Expressway, Zhengzhou-Shirenshan Expressway, and Xiangfan-Chongqing Railway. Positive technical and economic results were obtained. (CHEN Yongfeng, SHI Jianxin, LI Gaowang)

图1.32 西汉高速公路上膨胀土路堑边坡的浆砌片石满铺防护遭到破坏。

Fig1.32 Failure of masonry protection on cut slope of expansive soil along the Xihan Highway.

① 喷洒CMA膨胀土生态改性剂。

Montmorillonite Absorbent was sprayed to reduce the swelling of the expansive soil.

② 改性后深度约1m范围内的边坡土体基本消除了膨胀土的胀缩特性，土体强度提高，水稳性好，改性后边坡稳定。

Expansibility of the slope was suppressed within a depth of 1 m. The soil was strengthened, and the water content was stable, resulting in a stable slope.

③ 改性后的边坡土体能种植花草灌木，景观效果和耐久性均优于刚性防护。

Vegetation can be planted on the absorbent slope,yielding a better view and superior durability as compared to rigid protection measures.

图1.33 郑石高速公路采用膨胀土生态改性剂处治膨胀土路堑边坡。

Fig1.33 Montmorillonite Absorbent was used to treat expansive soil slopes along the Zhengzhou-Shirenshan Expressway.

第Ⅱ章 中国山区公路与铁路建设中的典型工程边坡

Chapter II Highway & Railway Engineered Slopes in Mountainous Area

中国是一个多山的国家，山地面积（含高原、丘陵在内）占全国土地面积的2/3。除上海外，各省市区均有山地分布，其中，贵州、云南、四川3省的山地占本省面积的90%～95%。

20世纪50年代以来，伴随着山区铁路与公路建设的发展，工程边坡的数量和规模逐步增加。尤其是20世纪末以来，中国山区高速公路的快速修建导致大量高边坡的出现。同时由于特殊的地形和地质环境，在建设中出现了较多的高边坡变形与破坏。

China is a mountainous country and the mountain area, including plateau and hilly area, occupies 2/3 of the country area. Mountain regions distribute almost all the provinces and districts except Shanghai. Among them, the mountains of Guizhou Province, Yunnan Province, Sichuan Province account for 90%~95% of their provincial areas.

From the 1950s, amounts and scales of engineering slopes increase gradually due to development of construction of road and railway in mountain regions. Especially from the end of the last century, quick construction of highway in the Chinese mountain regions led to occurrence of a large amount of high slopes. Many deformations and failures of high slopes occur during the construction due to the special landforms and geological environment.

中国典型山区公路、铁路项目一览表
Typical Highway & Railway Project in China Mountainous Area

编号 No.	项目名称 Project Name	长度 Length(km)	穿越的主要山脉 Main Mountains' Name along the Project
H01	四川至西藏公路 Sichuan—Tibet highway	2155	横断山 Hengduanshan Mountains[M1] 喜马拉雅山 Himalaya Mountains[M2] 念青唐古拉山 Nianqingtanggulashan Mountains[M3]
H02	新疆至西藏公路 Xinjiang—Tibet highway	2140	昆仑山 Kunlunshan Mountains[M4] 冈底斯山 Gangdisishan Mountains[M5]
H03	独山子到库车公路 Dushanzi—Kuche highway	560	天山 Tianshan Mountains[M6]
R01	宝鸡至成都铁路 Baoji—Chengdu railway	669	秦岭 Qinling Mountains[M7], 大巴山 Dabashan Mountains
H04	西安至汉中高速公路（陕西） Xi'an—Hanzhong expressway	255	
R02	南宁至昆明铁路 Nanning—Kunming railway	818	云贵高原 Yungui plateau[M8]
H05	京珠高速公路粤境北段 Northern Guangdong section of the Beijing—Zhuhai expressway	110	南岭 Nanling Mountains[M9]
H06	北京至福州高速公路福建段 Fujian section of the Beijing—Fuzhou expressway	220	闽浙丘陵 Minzhe hills[M10]
H07	徽（黄山）杭(州)高速公路安徽段 Anhui section of the Huangshan—Hangzhou expressway	82	昱岭（江南丘陵） Yuling Mountains (Jiangnan hills)[M11]
H08	元江至磨黑高速公路（云南） Yuanjiang—Mohei expressway	147	无量山 Wuliangshan Mountains, 哀牢山 Ailaoshan Mountains[M12]
H09	万州至梁平高速公路（重庆） Wanzhou—Liangping expressway	70	精华山（川东丘陵） Jinghuashan Mountains[M13]
H10	大同至运城高速公路（山西） Datong—Yuncheng expressway	666	恒山 Hengshan Mountain 吕梁山西麓 Luliangshan Mountains[M14]
H11	沪蓉西高速公路（湖北） Hubei section of the Shanghai—Chengdu expressway	320	武陵山 Wuling Mountains[M15]

注：表中上标M1～M15为主要山脉（地）在遥感影像图中的标注编号。

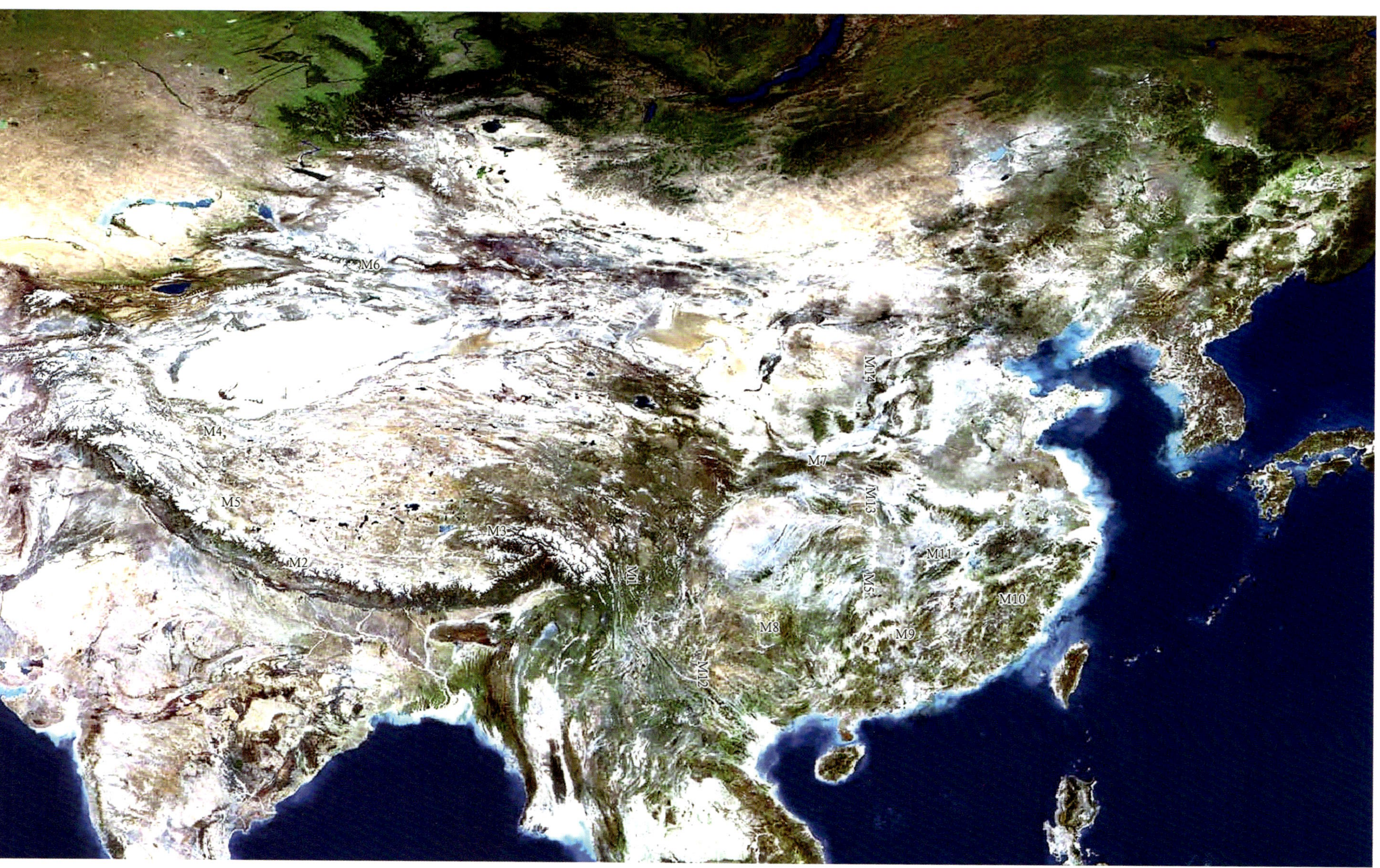

图 2.1 中国及周边地区遥感影像图

Fig.2.1 Remote Sensing Image of China and its Surrounding Areas

■（四）川（西）藏公路102滑坡群Ⅱ号滑坡整治工程

川藏公路102滑坡群位于雅鲁藏布江大转弯东北侧的峡谷地带，于1991年6月20日突然快速下滑，大量物质高速滑入江中，一度堰塞成湖，其后大坝溃决导致其他多个较大滑坡的形成和扩展，进而形成了举世闻名的"102滑坡群"。滑坡群影响路段长约3km，共有滑坡22处，其中以Ⅱ号滑坡（即102滑坡）的规模最大，曾多次造成车毁人亡的重大交通事故。Ⅱ号滑坡是发育在厚层冰碛台地前缘的大型堆积层滑坡，川藏公路从该滑坡的中下部通过。残留滑坡体呈不规则长方形，弧形后壁高60～90m，宽300m，前缘宽420m，剪出口在坡脚（江面）以上30m，滑体平均厚度30m，残留滑体$240 \times 10^4 m^3$。

Ⅱ号滑坡的整治以"减重卸载，锚固支挡，加强排水"为指导思想，主要工程措施包括：

(1)挖方减重卸载

对滑坡范围内残留的脊梁进行削坡卸载，挖方边坡采用阶梯形，每级边坡高10m，坡率1：1，边坡平台宽5m（8m、12m）。

(2)锚索挡墙路堤

在滑坡范围内的深切冲沟部位填筑路堤，对高度大于5m的填方边坡采用单级或多级锚索挡土墙支挡防护，最大防护高度38m。

(3)挖方边坡防护

采用锚杆挡土墙、锚索肋板墙、浆砌片石挡土墙等,对不稳定挖方边坡进行防护。防护高度为5～11m。

(4)综合排水

设置急流槽、山坡截水沟、平台截水沟、边沟等，疏导路基上侧冲沟和坡面水流、泥石流。

本工程边坡的主要特点和难点是在厚层冰碛物滑坡体上修筑路基，并在大型碎石土堆积层滑坡上实施大吨位土层锚索。在工程施工与后期运营期间，不间断地进行了地表位移、深部位移及结构物应力等一系列监测工作。

本工程边坡尽管是按临时性保通工程设计的，但自2002年11月完工直到目前为止，依然能够保证全年畅通。

图2.2 ① 滑坡未整治前的状况

The condition of the landslide before treatment

■ Treatment project for No.2 Landslide in the 102 Landslide Group in the Sichuan-Tibet Highway

The 102 landslide group along the Sichuan-Tibet Highway is located in the canyon zone to the northeast of the great turn of the Brahmaputra River. A massive and sudden landslide occurred on 20th June 1991 which dammed the river, forming a barrier lake. The subsequent collapse of the dam caused further landslides on a larger scale, which later became known worldwide as the "102

Landslide Group". There were 22 landslides along a 3km section of the highway. The No.2 Landslide was the largest and caused several fatal traffic accidents.

The No.2 landslide was a large deposit landslide generated in the foreland of the thick drift stratum, with the Sichuan-Tibet Highway cutting through its lower part. The remaining part of the landslide is shaped like an irregular rectangle, which is 300 m wide with a 60~90 m high curved scarp, and a foreland 420 m in width. The toe of the landslide is 30 m higher than the river level. The average thickness of the gliding mass is 30 m and the total volume of the remaining part is 240×10^4 m^3.

Treatments for the No.2 landslide include load reduction, anchored retaining walls as support, and drainage.

(1) Load reduction by excavation

The remaining ridge within the landslide was terraced. The height of each step is 10 m with a slope ratio of 1:1, and the width of the berms is 5 m (8 m, 12 m).

(2) Anchored retaining wall

Embankments were constructed in the deep gullies within the scope of the landslide. Single or multiple anchored retaining walls were built when the slope was higher than 5 m. The maximum height of reinforcement was 38 m.

(3) Protection of cut slope

Anchored retaining walls, anchor-line rib-board walls and mortared retaining walls were used to protect the cut slopes. The height of reinforcement was from 5 m to 11 m.

(4) Drainage

Quick flow slots, intercepting ditches and lateral ditches were used to drain the water and debris flows on slope surfaces and roadbases.

The main feature and difficulties involved in this project were the construction of embankments on the landslide in the thick drift stratum and the installation of large-tonnage anchors in the macadam landslide. Ground settlement, displacement and stress in structures were monitored continuously during the construction and service periods.

Though this project was primarily designed for temporary purposes, the highway has nevertheless remained unblocked since the completion of the project in November 2002.

图 2.2 ② 减重卸载后形成的上边坡 *The upper slope after load reduction by cutting*

各级边坡高度：第Ⅰ～Ⅶ级 10m，第Ⅷ级一坡到顶；各级坡率均采用 1∶1；平台宽度第Ⅰ～Ⅳ级、Ⅵ～Ⅶ级为 5m，第Ⅴ级 12m，第Ⅷ级 8m，平台采用 7.5 号浆砌片石铺砌。

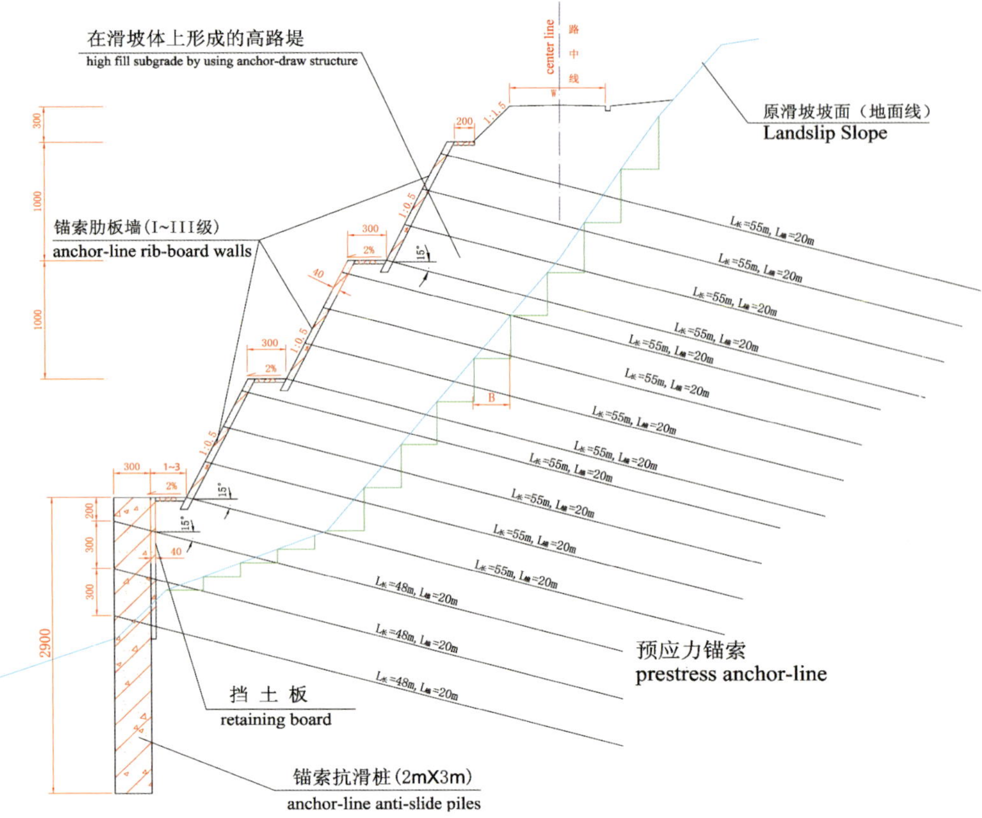

图 2.2 ③ 冲沟部位锚索挡墙路堤典型断面(尺寸单位: cm)

Typical section of the landslide(located in the gully)

图 2.2 ④ 边坡综合防护

Comprehensive slope protection

图2.2 ⑤ 下边坡三级锚索肋板墙

Arrangement of the prestressed cable rib-board wall on the lower slope

每级墙净高10m，胸坡1∶0.5，两级墙之间设3m宽平台，并以浆砌片石铺砌封面。肋柱截面70cm × 60cm，肋间板厚40cm，每片墙宽6m。墙体和肋柱均采用C25混凝土浇筑。预应力锚索长30～55m，设计荷载600kN。

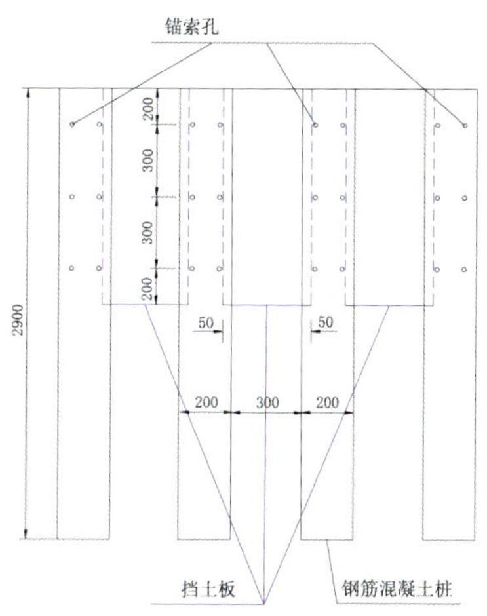

图2.2 ⑥ 坡脚预应力锚索桩板墙(尺寸单位: cm) *Sheet pile wall with prestressed cables at the toe of the slope*

设于边坡总高度超过30m的坡脚，钢筋混凝土桩截面2m × 3m，桩长29m，每根桩设6根锚索。预应力锚索长48m，设计荷载600kN。桩间设挡土板，板厚40cm。

The sheet-pile wall with prestressed cables is built at the slope toe with total height of over 30 m. The cross section areas of concrete piles are 2 m×3 m and their lengths are 29 m. Six anchors are built for each pile. Length of each prestressed anchor is 48 m and its design load is 600 kN. Breast boards are set between two piles and their thicknesses are 40 cm.

图2.2-⑦ 综合整治效果（通车后两年）

Effects of comprehensive treatment (two years in service)

■南（宁）昆（明）铁路八渡车站古滑坡治理工程

南昆铁路八渡车站滑坡位于贵州省册亨县南盘江北岸的八渡口，宽约360m，主轴长560m，厚20～40m，滑坡体积约420 × 10^4m^3，为一巨型切层古滑坡，线路在古滑坡中上部以挖方通过。1997年雨季连降暴雨，雨水大量下渗，线路右侧次级滑坡前部出现变形，同时深孔监测表明线路左侧主滑坡复活。八渡车站古滑坡复活，直接威胁已建成车站的安全和南昆铁路全线按时通车。经组织专家多方论证，决定在原位整治。

南昆铁路八渡车站滑坡，以其规模巨大，滑体深厚、破碎、富水及整治工程浩大而闻名。本工程以采用大量超长、超深预应力锚索、锚索桩、抗滑桩支挡及地下、地面排水为主，辅以清方减载及监测等手段，综合治理复杂地质条件下的大型滑坡，堪称铁路行业之最。采取的整治措施主要有：

(1)锚索桩和抗滑桩支挡，路线左侧设两排锚索抗滑桩共113根，右侧设三排抗滑桩共111根，平均桩长31m，最长55m，总计桩长6870m。

(2)预应力锚索加固，左侧两排锚索桩顶设锚索231根，右侧独立设置锚索132根，锚索总长20310m。平均索长56m，最长75m。

(3)地表、地下立体排水，线路两侧铺砌网状截、排水沟15条，共计5833m；两侧各设1.7m × 1.4m、1.9m × 1.9m地下泄水洞一座，总长843.93m。

(4)保护地质环境，清方减载，平顺坡面，恢复植被。

(5)全面、系统的动态监测，地表位移、深孔位移、锚索和锚索桩受力监测、桩身混凝土质量声波透视检测、地下水变化监测等。

整治工程施工期间不间断的地表变形和深孔位移监测表明：随着整治工程实施，变形趋于稳定，治理取得成效；随着工程的逐步完成，滑坡变形得到抑制。工程自正式交验至今，特别是经历了2000年、2001年较大暴雨后（滑坡点最大日降雨量达108mm），无变形迹象。整治工程竣工至今已经8年，监测数据几乎没有变化，表明滑坡整体处于稳定状态。

■Treatment project of the Badu Station Ancient Landslide along the Nanning-Kunming Railway

The ancient landslide at Badu station along the Nanning-Kunming railway is located at Badukou on the northern bank of the Nanpan River in Ceheng county of Guizhou Province. It is about 360 m wide, 24~40 m thick and the main axis is about 560 m long. The volume of the landslide is about 420 × 10^4 m^3. The railway passes through the upper part of the fossil landslide by cutting.

The ancient landslide was stable before the construction of this railway. But during the rainy seasons in1997, heavy rain led to deformation in the front part of the secondary landslide on the right-hand side of the line. Monitoring of deep soil indicated that the main fossil landslide on the left-hand side of the line had revived. The revival of the fossil landslide at Badu Station posed a direct threat to the safety of the existing station and the operation of the Nanning-Kunming railway. The Ministry of Railway thus organized experts to study the landslide and decided to treat it at its original site.

The treatment methods are as follows:

(1) Anchor cable pile and slope stabilizing pile retaining structure:113 anchored slope stabilizing piles were installed in two rows on the left-hand side of the railway, and 111 slope stabilizing piles installed in three rows on the right-hand side. The longest pile was about 55 m in length, the average and total lengths of the piles were 31 m and 6870 m respectively.

(2) Prestressed anchor cable: 231 and 132 anchor cables were installed on the left-and right-hand sides of the railway respectively. The total length of the anchor cables was 20310 m, with the longest being 75 m and the average length 56 m.

(3) Surface and underground drainage: Fifteen discharge ditches were laid in a mesh pattern on both sides of the rail, totalling 5833m in length. A 1.7 m×1.4 m and a 1.9 m×1.9 m discharge tunnel were built respectively on each side of the embankment. The total length of the tunnels was 843.93 m.

(4) Protection of geological environment: Loading was reduced, slopes were smoothened out, and vegetation was restored.

(5) Comprehensive and systematic monitoring of slope activity: Ground surface displacement, displacement of deep soil, stress on anchor cables and anchor cable piles, the quality of concrete shafts, and variations in underground water were monitored.

Continuous monitoring of ground surface deformation and displacement of deep soil during construction indicated that deformation was tending towards stability and the treatment was effective. With the gradual completion of the project, landslide deformation was brought under control. Since the completion of this project, there has been no sign of deformation, not even after heavy rainstorms in 2000 and 2001 (the maximum rainfall recorded for one single day reaching 108 mm). There has been little change in the monitored data over the past eight years since the completion of this project, indicating that slope is in a stable state in general.

图 2.3 ① 八渡古滑坡侧视（南盘江冲刷滑坡前缘）
Side view of Badu fossil landslide (the front edge of Badu fossil landslide washed by Nanpanjiang River)

图 2.3 ② 八渡车站滑坡整治工程全貌
Full view of treatment project for landslide at Badu Station

N
F_4
F_1
78°
普通桩
common piles
3号山梁锚索52孔
3# ridge, 52 anchor wire holes
2号山梁锚索80孔
2# ridge, 80 anchor wire holes
昆明
F_2 南宁
50°
货物站台
八渡站货物广场
platform of freight yard
支河
病害周界
boundary of unstable area
左侧第一排锚索桩
the first row of anchor wire pile on the left side
支河
左侧第二排锚索桩
the second row of anchor wire pile on the left side
F_3
65°
南 盘 江

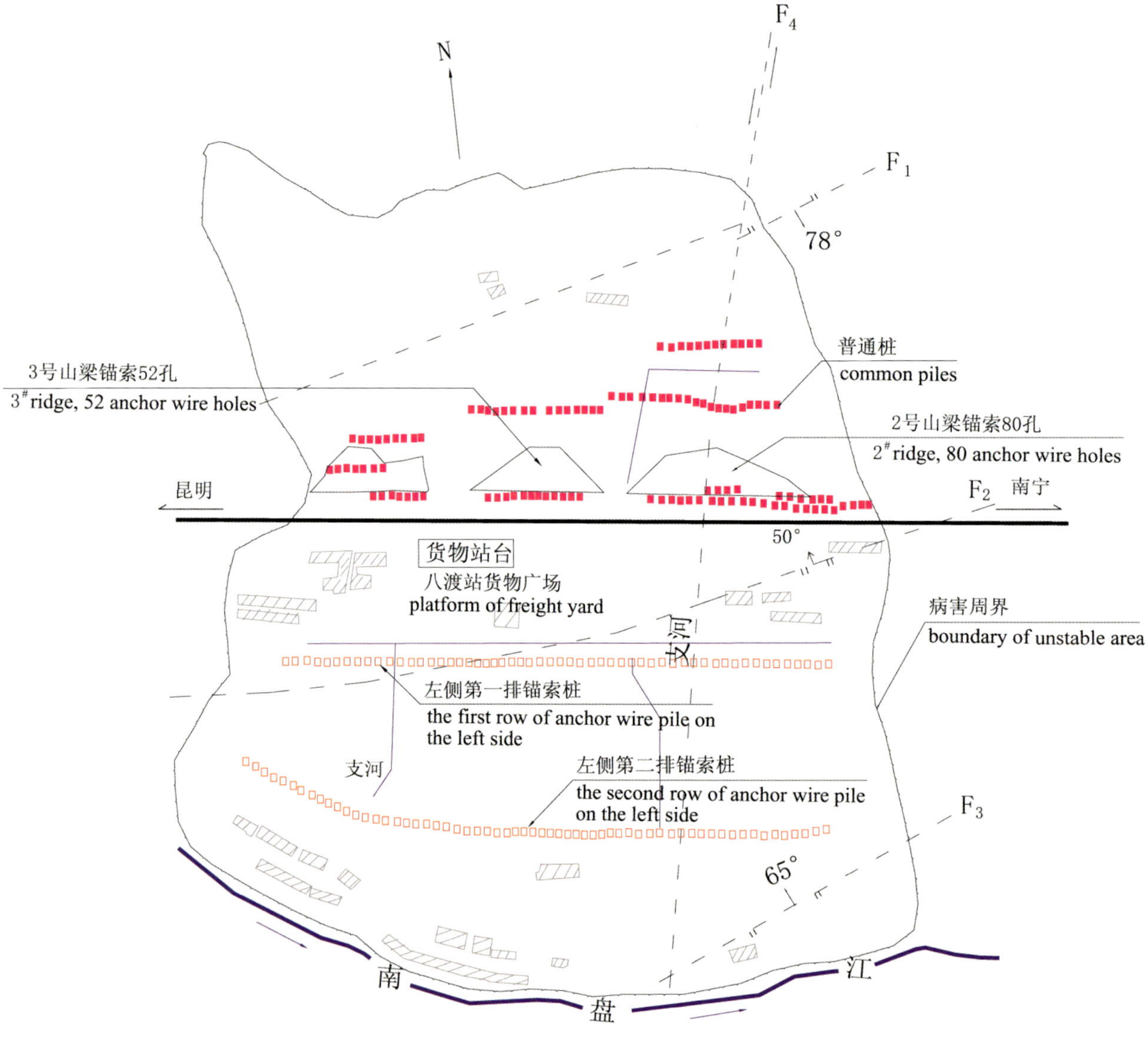

图 2.4 ① 八渡车站滑坡整治工程平面图 *Plan view of treatment project for landslide at Badu station*

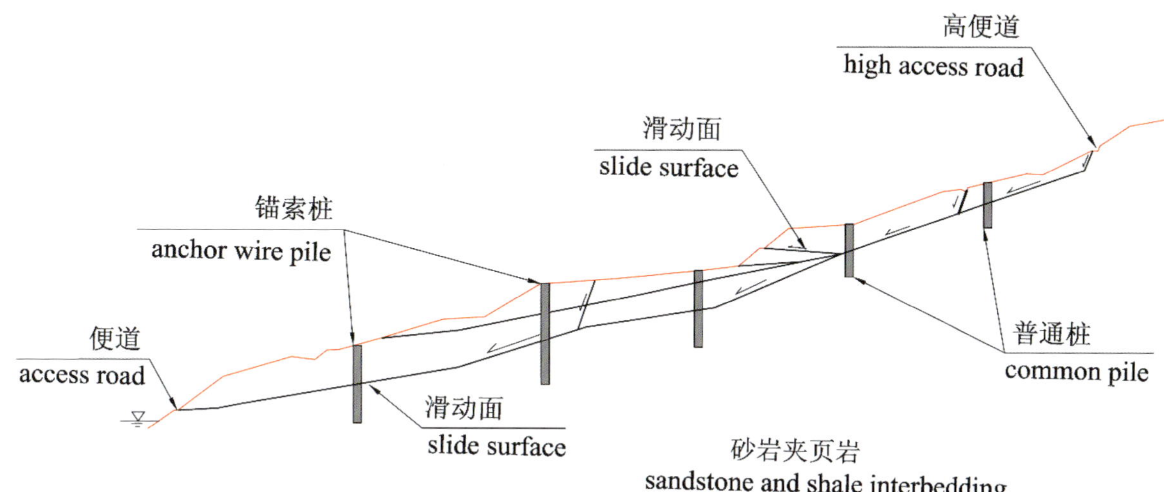

图 2.4 ② 八渡车站滑坡整治工程断面图

Cross-section of treatment project for landslide at Badu Station

图 2.5 ① 八渡车站站后锚索墩与右侧第一排抗滑桩

Reinforced pier with anchoring and slope stabilizing pile at the back of Badu station

图 2.5② 八渡车站临江侧（左侧第二排）预应力锚索抗滑桩

共 59 根，平均桩长 31m，桩间距 7m，桩截面 (2 ~ 2.5)m × (2.5 ~ 4)m，桩锚入滑面以下岩层的长度 10 ~ 14m。

Prestressed cable slope stabilizing pile on side of river near the station

Totally 59 prestressed anchorage slope stabilizing piles are built on the river side of the Badu Station. The average length of piles is 31 m and the pile spacing is 7 m. The cross section areas of piles are (2~2.5) m×(2.5~4) m. The depths of piles anchor into the rock under the sliding surface are 10 ~ 14 m.

图 2.5③　地下泄水洞出口

Exit of the drainage tunnel

■（四）川（西）藏公路中坝段溜沙坡整治工程

溜沙坡是陡峭坡面基岩的寒冻风化产物在重力作用下汇集到坡脚堆积而成的动态临界平衡的砂粒粒级岩屑坡。川藏公路中坝段是溜沙坡最具代表性的地段。在长约26km的路段集中分布溜沙坡18处。坡面高度多在200～300m，天然休止角小于35°。粒度组成几乎不含黏粒。溜沙坡坡面上大量的碎屑岩块持续不断地崩坍滑落，堆积掩埋公路，对川藏公路的畅通构成严重威胁。

中坝段溜少坡防治采取的主要措施包括：圆木框格、土工格室、SNS柔性防护网等坡面防护工程；坡脚挡墙拦挡工程；明洞遮挡工程。(唐良健、张正波等提供)

■Treatment project of Sand-sliding Landslide in the Sichuan-Tibet Highway

A sand-sliding slope is formed when the surface of a steep slope is weathered and the product under the effect of gravity gathers at the toe of the slope, creating a slope in a dynamic critical equilibrium state.The sand-sliding slope in the Zhongba section is a typical example of such slopes.There are 18 sand-sliding slopes distributed along a 26 km section of the highway. Most of the slopes range from 200 m to 300 m in height, and their rest angles are less than 35° . No clay particle is found. Continual avalanches bringing with them large quantities of rock mass buried the highway and posed a serious threat to its unimpeded use.

The main treatments for the Zhongba section included timber frames, geocells and SNS soft prevention nets for slope surface protection, retaining walls at slopes toes and open cave barriers. (TANG Liangjian, ZHANG Zhengbo)

图 2.6　利用坡脚挡墙的拦挡作用，防止溜沙直接流入公路威胁过往车辆、行人安全。

Fig 2.6　Sand-sliding is prevented by the retaining wall.

图 2.7　圆木框格＋坡脚挡墙综合防护溜沙坡坡面

Fig 2.7　Slope protection by lattice girder of timber and gravity retaining wall

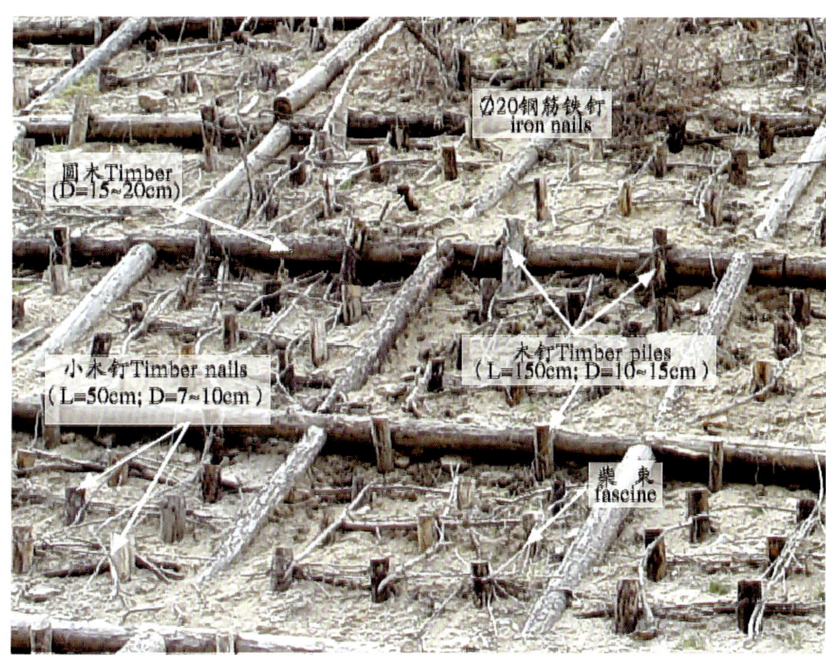

图 2.8　圆木框格布置

Fig 2.8 Arrangement of lattice girder using timbers

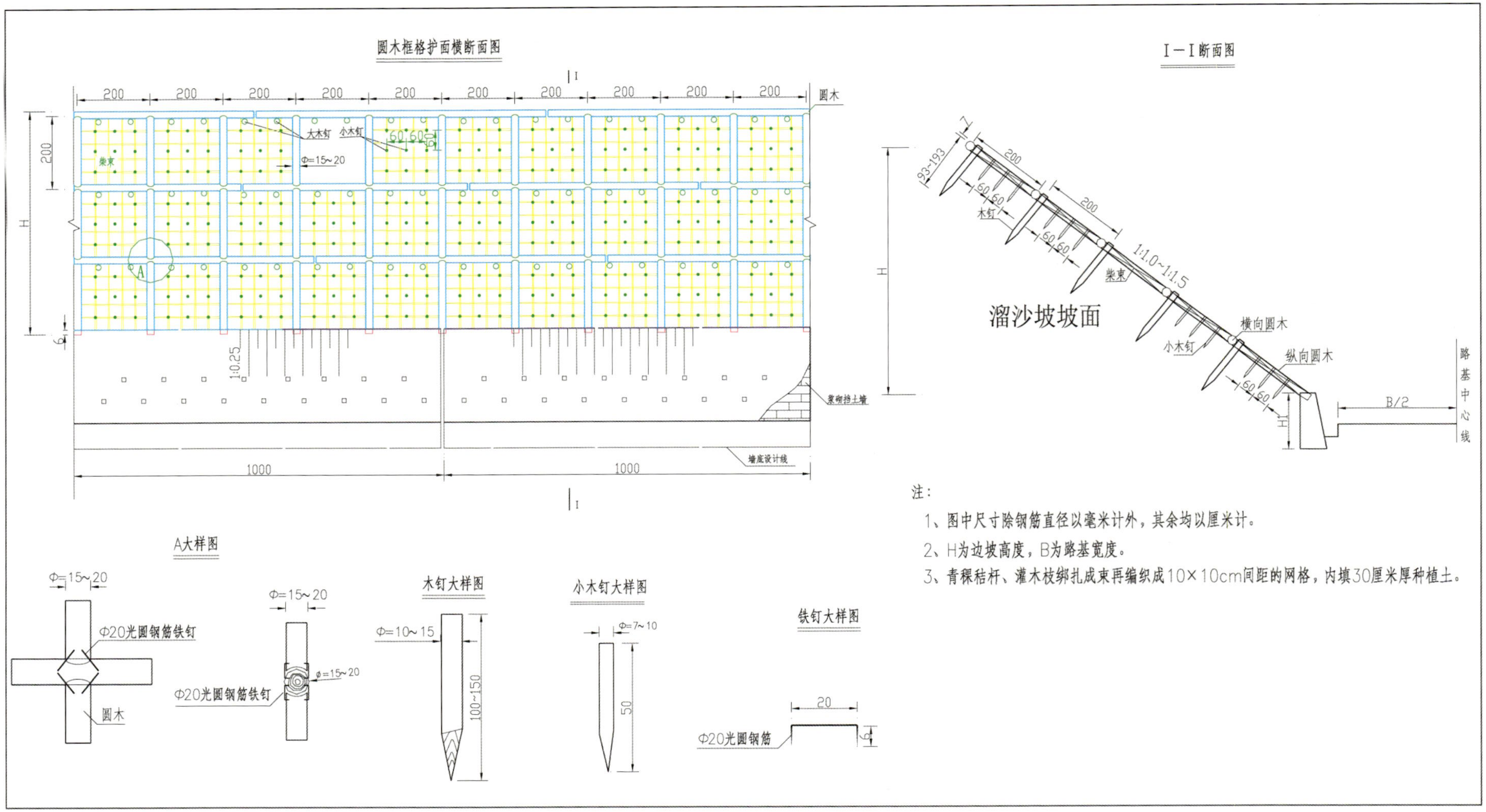

圆木框格护面横断面图

200 200 200 200 200 200 200 200 200 200

圆木

大木钉　小木钉　柴束　Φ=15~20　60 60 50

H　200　6　1:0.25

浆砌挡土墙　墙底设计线

1000　1000

I—I断面图

93~193　7　200　200　60 60　木钉　1:1.0~1:1.5　柴束　横向圆木　小木钉　纵向圆木

溜沙坡坡面

H　B/2　路基中心线

注：

1、图中尺寸除钢筋直径以毫米计外，其余均以厘米计。

2、H为边坡高度，B为路基宽度。

3、青稞秸杆、灌木枝绑扎成束再编织成10×10cm间距的网格，内填30厘米厚种植土。

A大样图

Φ=15~20　Φ20光圆钢筋铁钉　圆木　Φ=15~20　Φ20光圆钢筋铁钉　φ=15~20

木钉大样图

Φ=10~15　100~150

小木钉大样图

Φ=7~10　50

铁钉大样图

20　6　Φ20光圆钢筋

图 2.9　圆木框格护坡设计图　　*Fig 2.9　Layout of timber lattice girder*

图 2.10① 采用特制的细篦式SNS柔性防护网可有效阻止溜沙坡表面沙石的流动

The fine slotted SNS soft prevention net could prevent the sliding of the rock debris

图 2.10② 对流砂面高陡，边坡稳定性差，断通阻车严重路段采用明洞保护公路

Open cave barriers are adopted in sections where slopes are steep, unstable and prone to serious road blockage

■重庆万（州）梁（平）高速公路沿线的典型边坡工程

万梁高速公路全长约70km，位于四川盆地东北边缘的中低山丘陵区，山高坡陡、沟壑纵横，高填、深挖、高桥、长隧相连，其中有20km路段穿越砂、泥岩顺层地段。建设期间共发生滑坡、高边坡病害70余处，主要为顺倾层状高边坡、大型堆积层滑坡，著名的工点有张家坪大型堆积层滑坡及大荒田、安龙顺层高边坡等。

针对沿线地质病害的复杂性、频发性和病害类型的多样性，开展了“万梁高速公路沿线高边坡病害和大型滑坡发生发展及防治技术研究”，通过系统研究高边坡病害产生的地质条件、坡体结构特征和变形破坏类型，利用“减、锚、挡、固、疏”等综合治理技术，成功地治理了公路建设中发生各类边坡病害，其中张家坪滑坡治理工程被专家誉为“国内高速公路滑坡治理最成功的项目之一”。

■Typical Engineered Slope in Wanzhou-Liangping Highway

Located in the low and middle hilly areas in the northeastern part of the Sichuan Basin, the Wanzhou-Liangping Highway is 70 km in length. A 20 km section of the highway passes through the bedding sandstone and mudstone sections. During the construction period, there were about 70 slope failures, most of which were high bedding slides and large-scale accumulative formation slides. The most well known slides included the Zhangjiaping (accumulative formation slide), Dahuangtian and Anlong (high bedding) slides.

In view of the complexity, frequency and diversity in type of slope failure along the highway, technological research on slope failure, the occurrence and development of large-scale landslides and their prevention was begun. Through a systematic study of geological conditions, features of slope structure and the types of failure, and by means of load reduction, anchoring, retaining walls, reinforcement and drainage, positive results were achieved in the treatment of various types of slope failures during road construction. Among the various projects, the Zhangjiaping Landslide Project is hailed by engineering professionals as “one of the most successful highway landslide treatment projects in China”.

图 2.11　竣工通车后的万梁高速公路

Fig 2.11 The Wanzhou-Liangping Highway in service

■疏挡结合治理的张家坪滑坡

该滑坡位于万梁高速公路K34+600～K35+000段右坡，是一个多级、多层的大型复杂堆积层老滑坡。滑坡分上、中、下三级，中级滑坡有浅、中、深三层滑带，按滑动方向的差异又分为两块。整个张家坪滑坡的深层滑带是基岩顶部的残坡积层，滑体约260 × 10^4m^3。滑坡变形的机理是崩坡积堆积物在地下水的长期作用下逐步转换为滑坡，受到地形地貌和基岩岩性软硬的限制，发育为多层多级的大型滑坡。滑动的主因是在中前部开挖路基，切除滑坡的前部支撑，引起老滑坡局部复活，继而引起滑坡中浅层整体复活。

张家坪滑坡规模大，分块、分级多，且地下水对滑坡的复活起了至关重要的作用，因此其治理工程遵循了“截排水为主、支挡为辅”和“统一规划、分期实施”的原则。张家坪滑坡共设置3排抗滑桩，中级滑坡后缘设置截排水盲洞等主体工程。首先实施路基两侧的抗滑桩和盲洞，中级滑坡后部第三排抗滑桩视第一批抗滑工程效果再决定。

考虑到地下水对张家坪滑坡的复活起着至关重要的作用，所以采取了渗水隧洞、斜孔排水等截、排水工程，以此减弱或消除地下水对滑坡的不利影响。

为验证滑坡发生、发展的机理，检验治理工程的效果，采取了深孔位移监测、地表位移监测等多种测试手段对滑坡治理进行了全程监测。监测结果表明，第一批抗滑工程完工后，经过两个雨季的考验，滑坡逐步趋于稳定。泄水盲洞和高速公路边仰斜排水孔起到了很大作用，盲洞平均出水量为7～$8m^3/d$。

■Retaining wall and drainage system in Zhangjiaping landslide

The Zhangjiaping landslide is located on the right-hand slope in the K34+600~K35+000 section along the Wanzhou-Liangping highway. It is a large, complex, multilevel and multilayer accumulative formation ancient landslide. It is divided into the upper, middle and lower levels. The middle level has three sliding zones (shallow, middle and deep), which further divides into two parts based on the direction of the slide. The deep sliding zone of the Zhangjiaping landslide is the residual layer of the weathered top of the base rock, with a total volume of 260 × 10^4 m^3. Slope deformation developed as a result of long-term action of groundwater on the deposit, which gradually transformed itself into a landslide. Determined by the relief and topographical features as well as the degree of hardness of the base rock, the landslide developed into a multilevel and multilayer large-scale landslide. The main cause for the landslide was excavation during construction of the embankment, and the cutting of the slope toe, which contributed to the partial revival of the ancient landslide and subsequently to the general revival of the entire shallow layer.

The Zhangjiaping landslide was massive with multiple sections. As the effect of groundwater was crucial, the treatment projects upheld the principles of “drainage as the primary measure, support as secondary measures”, and “integrated planning and implementation in stages”. Three rows of slope stabilizing piles were installed; main installations such as drainage blind caves were installed at the back of the middle level. The slope stabilizing piles and blind caves on both sides of the embankment were implemented first; the implementation of the third row of slope stabilizing piles at the back of the middle level of the landslide would depend on the results obtained for the first batch of piles.

Considering the key role of groundwater in the revival of the landslide, tunnels and inclined holes were adopted for drainage to reduce the action of groundwater.

Displacement of deep soil and ground settlement were monitored during the whole treatment project. Monitored data indicated that the landslide was becoming stable after two rainy seasons after the installation of the first set of antiskid piles. Blind caves and draining holes at the side of the highway were highly effective as a drainage system and the water discharge volume was 7~8 m^3/d.

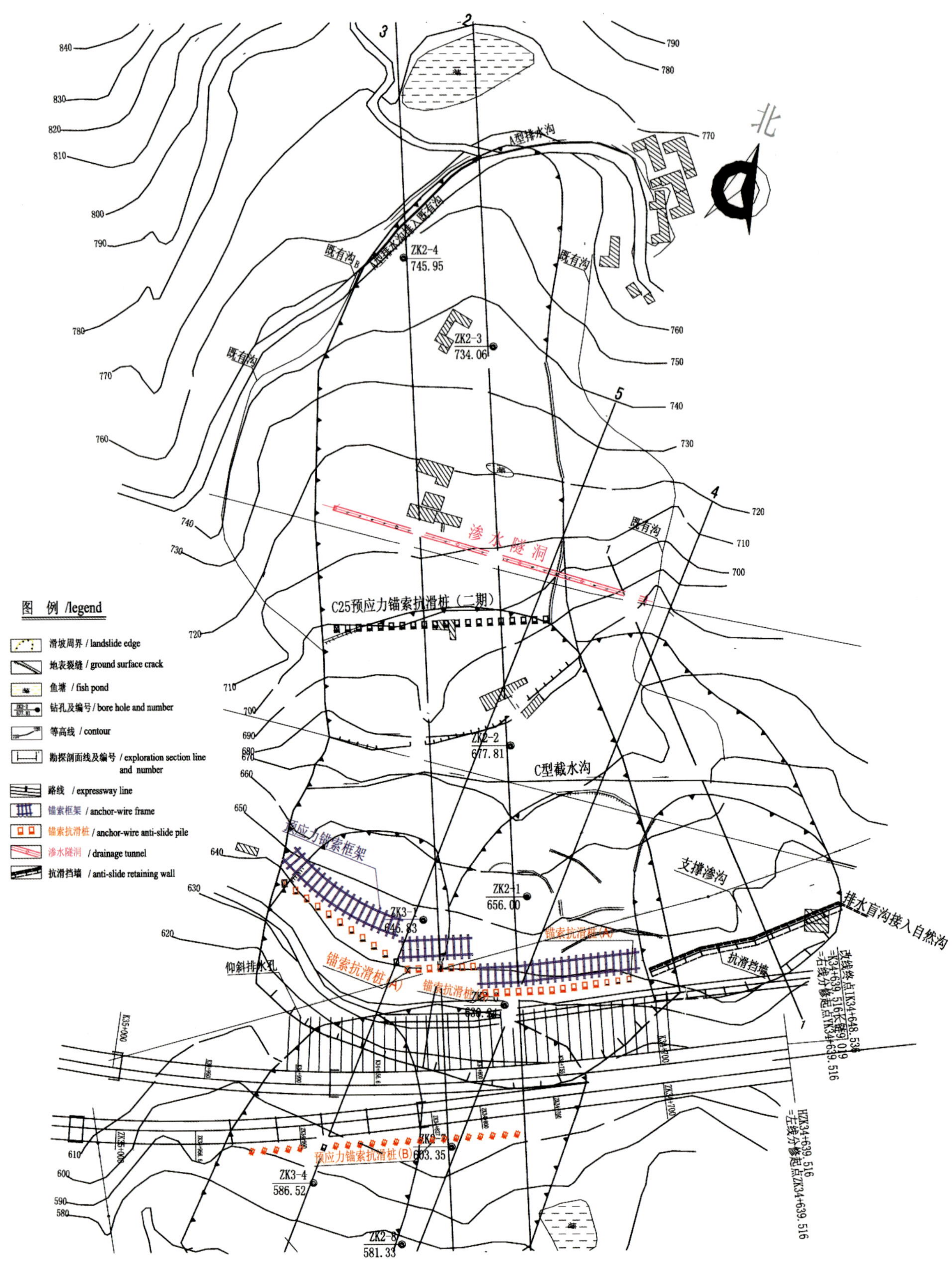

图 2.12　张家坪滑坡治理工程平面图

Fig 2.12 Plan view of Zhangjiaping landslide treatment project

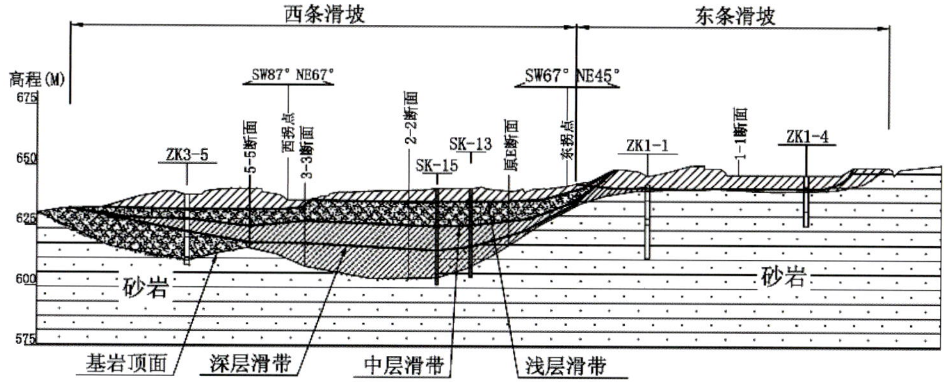

图 2.13 张家坪滑坡中级分条、分块断面示意图

Fig 2.13 Schematic plan of middle-grade sliding in Zhangjiaping landslide

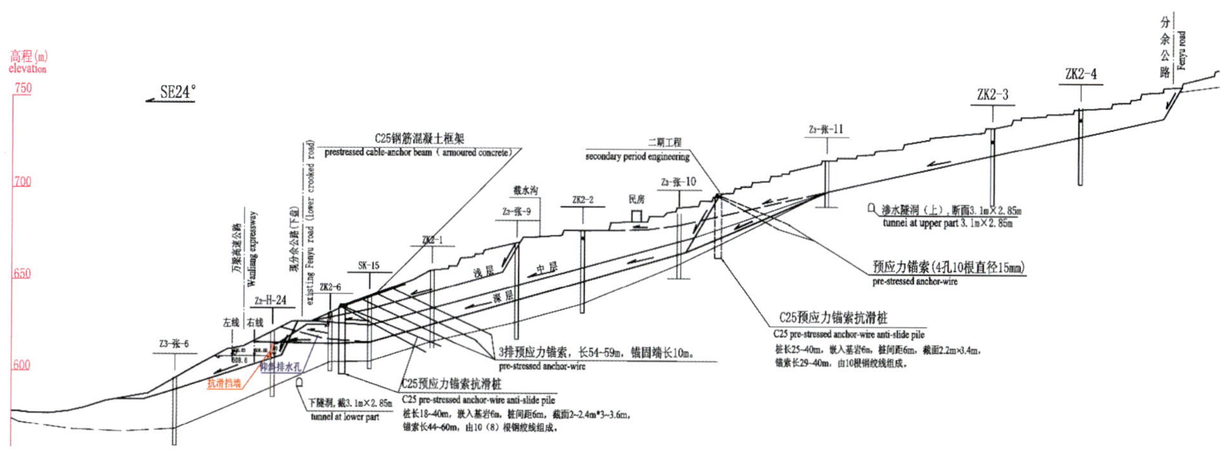

图 2.14 张家坪滑坡整治工程断面图（中级滑坡）

Fig 2.14 Cross-section of Zhangjiaping landslide treatment project(middle-grade landslide)

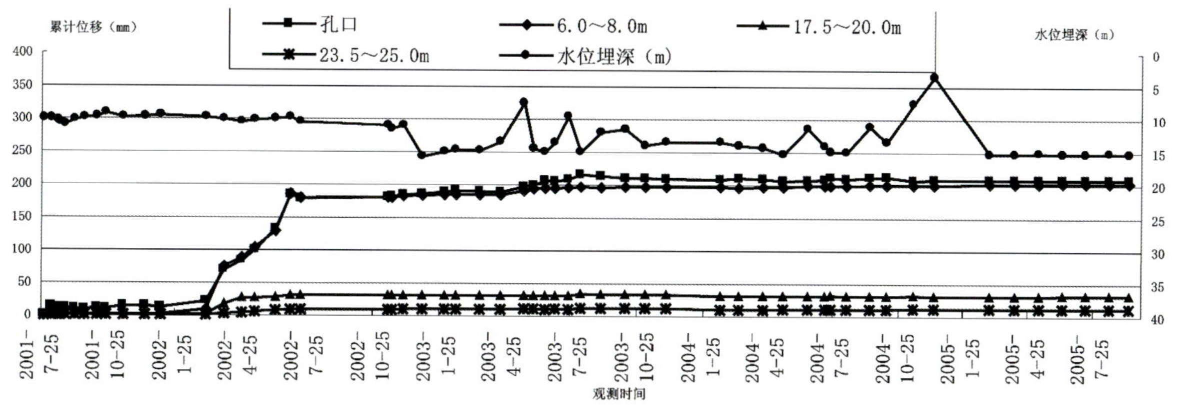

图 2.15 滑坡位移监测结果（位移－时间曲线）

Fig 2.15 Monitored result of landslide displacement(curve of displacement to time)

■分级开挖、分级稳定治理的大荒田滑坡

该滑坡为一顺层岩石滑坡，即强风化的泥岩组成的滑体沿其下伏的黑褐色的炭质页岩顶面滑动。采用了与边坡逐级开挖施工相协调的以预应力锚固（锚梁、锚墩）为主的主动治理工程措施。在第Ⅳ级及第Ⅲ级边坡上布设预应力锚地梁63根，在第Ⅰ、Ⅱ级边坡上布设预应力锚墩261个，在出水较多的第Ⅳ级边坡上布设一排20孔仰斜排水孔。

■Treatment of Dahuangtian Landslide: a treatment plan implemented in stages

The Dahuangtian Landslide is a bedding rock slope formed by the sliding of the highly weathered mudstone along the top of black-brown wacker. The proactive method of prestressed anchor reinforcement (anchor cable and anchor rob) was heavily used in tandem with the cutting of the slopes in steps. Sixty three prestressed anchor ground-beams were arranged in Sections IV and III, and 261 anchor piers were used along Sections I and II. Twenty drainage holes were installed along section IV.

图 2.16　治理后的张家坪滑坡全貌

Fig 2.16 An overview of Zhangjiaping landslide after treatment

图 2.17　大荒田滑坡治理工程

Fig 2.17 Treatment of Dahuangtian landslide

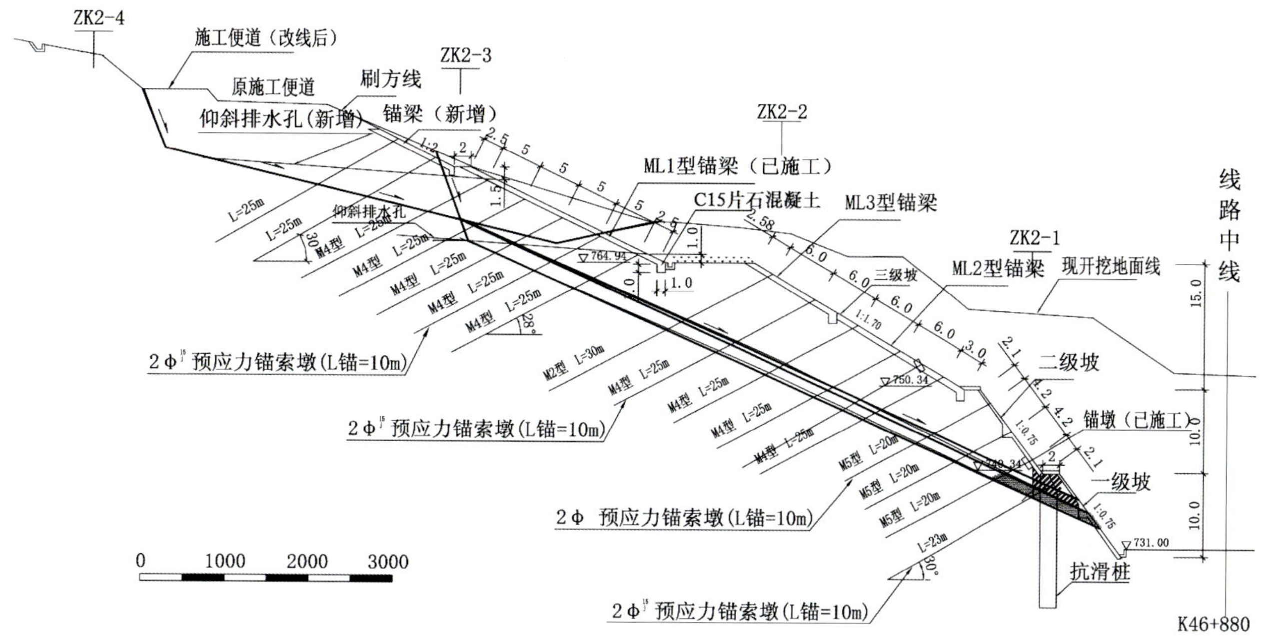

图 2.18 大荒田滑坡治理工程典型断面图(尺寸单位：m)
Fig 2.18 A typical cross-section of the treatment at the Dahuangtian landslide

① 桩－锚结构治理隧道出口滑坡
Pile-anchor at the exit of a tunnel

② 采用锚索框架加固高路堤
Reinforcing the embankment by reinforced concrete frame with anchoring

③ 悬臂抗滑桩治理隧道进口高路堤滑坡
Cantilever slope stabilizing piles used at the entrance of a tunnel

④ 锚索地梁与仰斜排水相结合治理滑坡
Anchored foundation beam and drainage system

图 2.19 其他典型治理工程结构 *Fig 2.19 Other typical structures used in the treatment*

■元（江）磨（黑）高速公路沿线的典型边坡工程

元磨高速公路全长147km，位于自然横坡陡峻的滇西高山峡谷地带。全线75%的线路布设于陡峻的谷坡之上，形成了路基挖方量大、路堑边坡高而密的特点。全线垂直高度大于30m的路堑边坡达349段，其中高于50m的有199段，高于100m的有66段，最高边坡的垂直高度为196m。

由于沿线地形地质条件极为复杂，工程建设中还曾发生滑坡、崩塌等边坡变形病害177处。边坡病害中以滑坡为主，约占70%。滑坡中有残积土滑坡37处、坡洪积土滑坡22处、特殊土滑坡5处，其余为岩石滑坡。

高边坡病害治理的工程结构类型主要有：抗滑桩、桩板墙、锚索抗滑桩、锚索框架梁、锚索地梁、挡墙、平孔排水等。高边坡加固及滑坡处治增加投资约5亿元。

典型工程边坡工点有：采用“多级锚固”治理的K259坍塌性滑坡和采用“注浆钢锚管框架”加固的K235高陡边坡等。

■ Typical Slope project in Yuanjiang-Mohei Highway

Located in the cliff canyon zone in the western part of Yunnan Province, the Yuanjiang-Mohei highway is 147 kilometers long. Seventy-five percent of the highway is found on steep slopes, requiring massive excavations and forming steep road-slopes. This highway has 349 road-slopes higher than 30 m, and among these, 199 are higher than 50 m, and 66 are higher than 100 m. The maximum height is 196 m.

Due to the complexity of the geological conditions along the highway, there were 177 slope deformations and failures during its construction. Of the failures, 70% were landslides. Among the landslides, 37 were residual soil slopes, 22 were diluvian soil slopes and 5 were special soil slopes. The remaining landslides were rock slopes.

The main structures for landslide treatment include slope stabilizing piles, pile-board walls, slope stabilizing piles reinforced with anchors, anchor frame beams, anchor ground-beams, retaining walls and drainage by plain holes. The total investment amount was approximately RMB500 million.

Typical engineered slope projects include the treatment of slumping slope at K259 using multiple anchors and injected anchor framing for the high and cliff slope at K235.

图2.20 元（江）磨（黑）高速公路沿线的典型边坡工程

Fig 2.20 Typical engineered slopes in Yuanjiang-Mohei expressway

■采用“多级锚固”治理的K259坍塌性滑坡

位于三公箐隧道进口左侧明洞接长部分，滑体主要由强风化破碎泥质砂岩组成，为一处由构造面控制的坍塌性滑坡。隧道进口左线山侧仰坡本是一沿自然冲沟向路线右侧滑动的堆积层老滑坡，因明洞开挖致使老滑坡复活。老堆积层滑坡复活后，采取接长明洞继续开挖坡脚又诱发了两次基岩切层坍滑（先坍塌后滑移），新生坍塌性基岩切层滑坡的滑动，牵动了仰坡堆积层老滑坡的再次复活。随后因清刷表层坍塌与滑动的松散岩土，增大了边坡的刷方高度，形成高近120m的高大边坡。

滑坡主要采取多级锚索框架和锚杆框架治理，主要措施包括：

(1)预应力锚索框架，Ⅱ、Ⅲ、Ⅴ、Ⅷ、Ⅸ级边坡上采用预应力锚索框架。

(2)锚杆框架，Ⅰ级和Ⅳ级边坡上采用了短锚杆的锚杆框架加固。

(3)坡面防护，Ⅰ级边坡锚杆框架内采用六棱砖覆土植草防护，Ⅵ级边坡采用拱形骨架防护，Ⅹ级及以上刷方边坡采用三维网植草防护，其余骨架和框架内采用喷播植草。

(4)地表水和地下水治理，地表设置完善的排水系统，Ⅰ级边坡和出水的边坡上灵活布设仰斜孔。

■ Using the multi-anchor to control slope at K259

In the connecting part between the open cave at the left entrance of the Sangongqing tunnel, the slope was formed from highly weathered mudstone, having collapsed due to the structural planes. The open cave of the entrance to the tunnel caused the revival of the ancient slope on the left-hand side of the entrance, and two more collapses in the base rock during the excavation of the open cave. A large high (near 120 m) slope was formed upon the removal of the loose topsoil.

Multiple anchor wire frame and anchor rod were the main treatment in this landslide.

(1)Prestressed anchor wire framing was mainly used in the slope sections of Ⅱ、Ⅲ、Ⅴ、Ⅷ、Ⅸ.

(2)Anchor rod frames were installed in the sections of I and IV.

(3)Protection of slope surface: seeding protection with six-rowed brick frames in sectionI, arched frame protection in section VI, three-dimensional seeding protection in section X, and seed spray-planting in the rest of the frames.

(4)Treatment of surface water and groundwater flow: a robust drainage system was installed on the ground surface. Inclined holes were installed in section Ⅰ and other water-yielding slope surfaces.

图2.21① 隧道明洞开挖前的边坡状况 *View of slope before cutting*

图2.21② 施工过程中，坍塌性滑坡从半坡滑出，掩埋前部公路及明洞，施工被迫暂时停止。

Slope slipped down during construction and buried the highway and a cave. The construction was suspended temporarily.

图2.21③ 新生切层滑坡与老堆积层滑坡并为一体，在平面上构成三角形滑坡形状，整个滑坡呈悬挂状、顺时针旋转滑动。

The new slope merged with the old accumulative landslide, forming a triangular-shaped landslide moving in a clockwise direction. The entire landslide resembles a hanging slope.

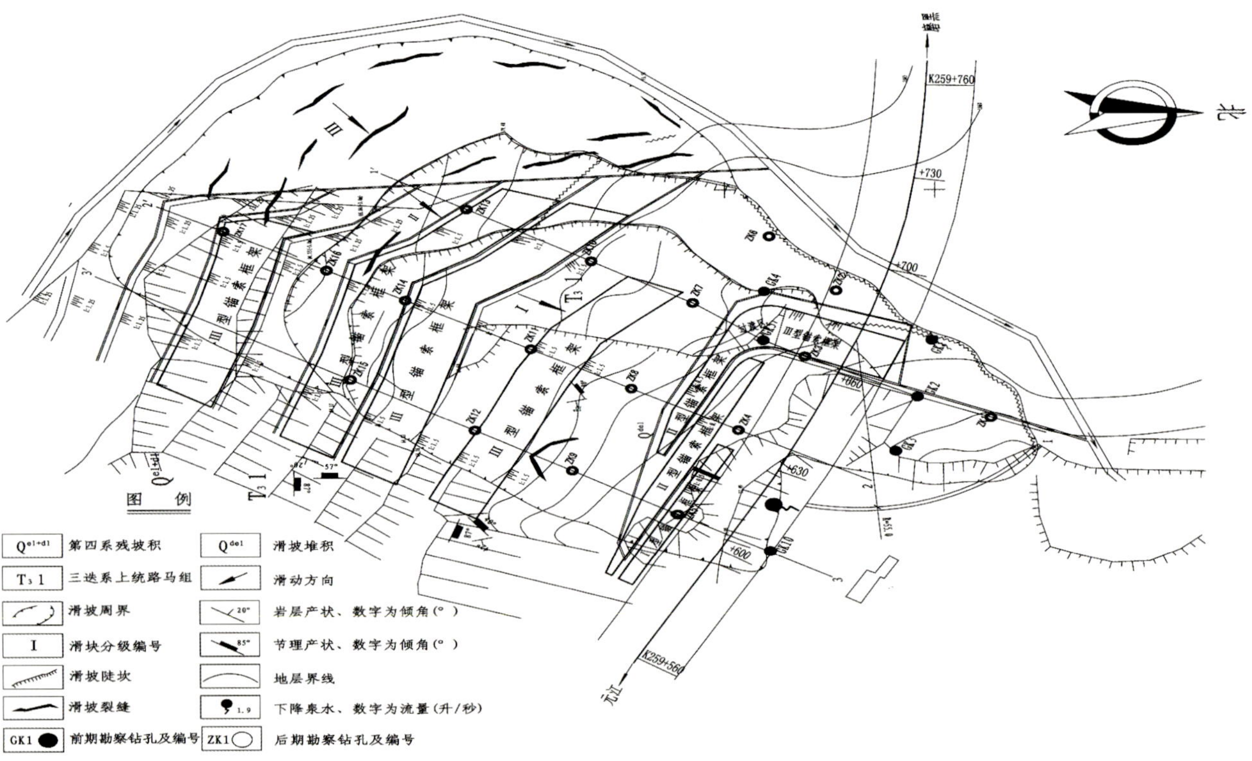

图 2.22 K259坍塌性滑坡治理工程平面布置图

Fig 2.22 Layout of the treatment project at the collapsed slope at K259

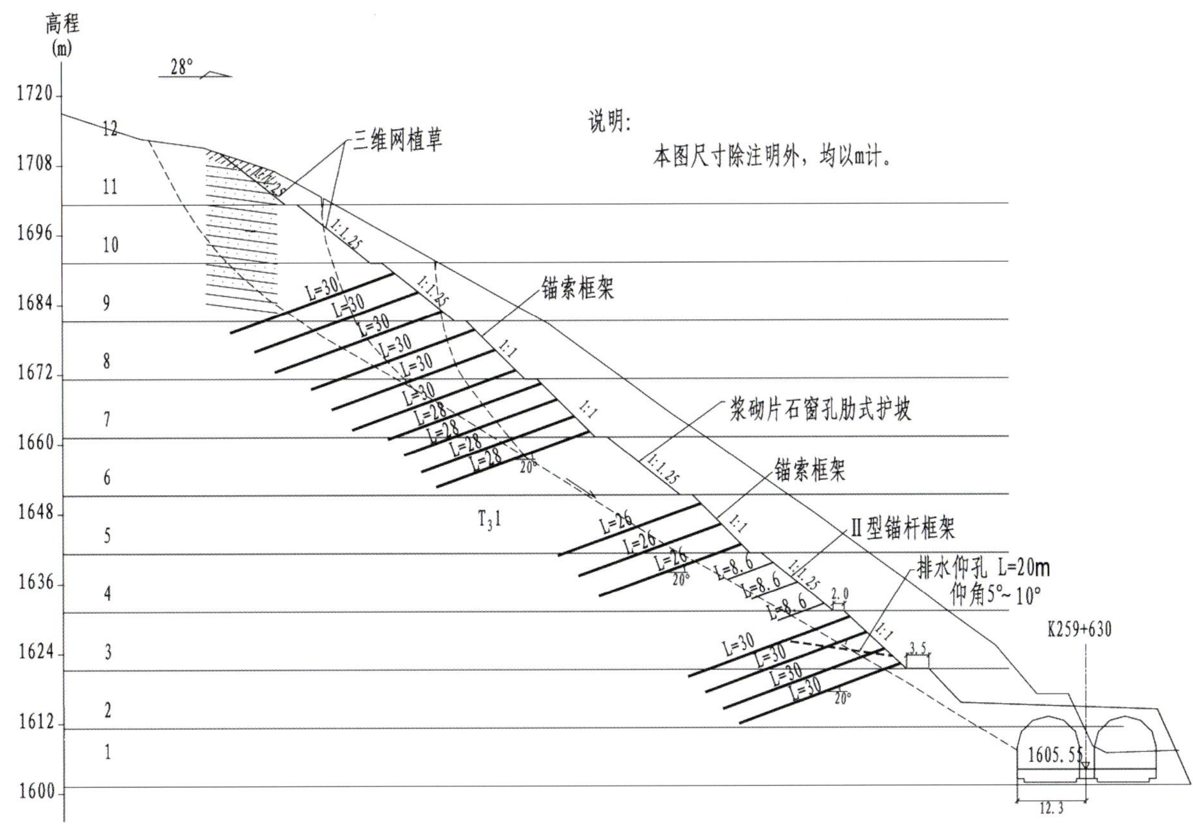

图2.23 K259坍塌性滑坡治理典型断面图

Fig 2.23 A typical cross-section of the treatment at the collapsed slope at K259

图 2.24 K259 高边坡及坍塌性滑坡治理竣工后全貌

Fig 2.24 Full view of the collapsed slope after treatment at K259

■ “注浆钢锚管框架”加固的K235高陡边坡

边坡位于K235+160～+600段路线右侧，边坡岩体表层为第四系残积层砂性粉质黏土，厚1～3m，其下为强风化花岗片麻岩，厚5～15m。坍塌病害产生以前（2002年），边坡最大高度163m，共18级，每级边坡坡率1∶0.75，高810m，最顶一级20m，防治措施为：I级边坡采用浆砌片石护面墙，其余各级边坡采用窗孔肋式浆砌片石护坡，VIII～XVII级边坡间隔采用锚索地梁加固。2003年1月12日，于K235+480～+550段VI级边坡以上发生了大规模坍塌。变形体堆落于已开挖到位的路基面上，破坏了多条已施工的锚索地梁。为避免更大规模的边坡病害发生，不得不对破环部分重新进行加固，并首次应用了预应力钢锚管框架注浆技术治理大型坍塌体，其主要措施有：

(1)注浆钢锚管框架，在刷方地段，VI～XⅦ级坡采用预应力注浆钢锚管框架加固。钢锚管采用预应力中空注浆锚杆定型产品，锚杆型号MZ51，规格Φ 51 × 7mm，抗拉强度550～600MPa。框架采用钢筋混凝土框架。

(2)预应力锚索框架及锚杆框架，XⅧ坡下半部采用预应力锚索框架加固，XⅧ级上半部及VI～XⅦ级坡中没有设置钢锚管注浆锚杆框架的边坡，采用钢筋锚杆框架加固，防止浅层变形。

(3)坡面防护，框架内采用三维网喷播植草防护。

■ Reinforcement of the Cliff Slope at K235 with Injected Steel Anchor-tube Frame

This landslide is located to the right of section K235+160~ K235+600. The topsoil of the landslide constitutes Quaternary sandy silty clay with 1 m to 3 m in thickness. Beneath the clay is highly weathered granite gneissose measuring 5 m to 15 m in thickness. Before the collapse in 2002, the slope measured 163 m at its highest point, was divided into 18 sections with a slope ratio of 1:0.75 with the topmost section being 20 m high. It was protected by several measures: section Ⅰ used mortared work, and sections VIII~X VII used anchor wire ground-beams and the rest of the sections used aperture rib coffer work. In Jan. 2003, a large-scale land slide occurred at section Ⅵ of section K235+480~+550, which destroyed several ground beams. To prevent any further large-scale slope failures, renewed reinforcement was applied and the injected prestressed steel anchor-tube was used for the first time. The main treatment included the following methods.

(1)Injected steel anchor-tube frame:This treatment was used in the slope sections of VI~X VII. The model of the anchor rod is MZ51 at a scale of Φ51×7 mm. The strength of extension was 550~600 MPa. The frame was built with reinforced concrete.

(2)Prestressed anchor wire frame and anchor rod frame:The prestressed anchor wire frame was used in the lower part of the slope sections of X and VIII, while the anchor rod frame was used in the upper part of the slope sections of X and VIII and the slope sections of VI~X VII to prevent deformation in shallow slopes.

(3)Pretection of slope surface:Seeds were planted in the three-dimensional protection nets.

图 2.25 K235高边坡及K235+480~+550段大型坍塌体

Fig 2.25 Massive collapse on a high slope between K235+480~+550

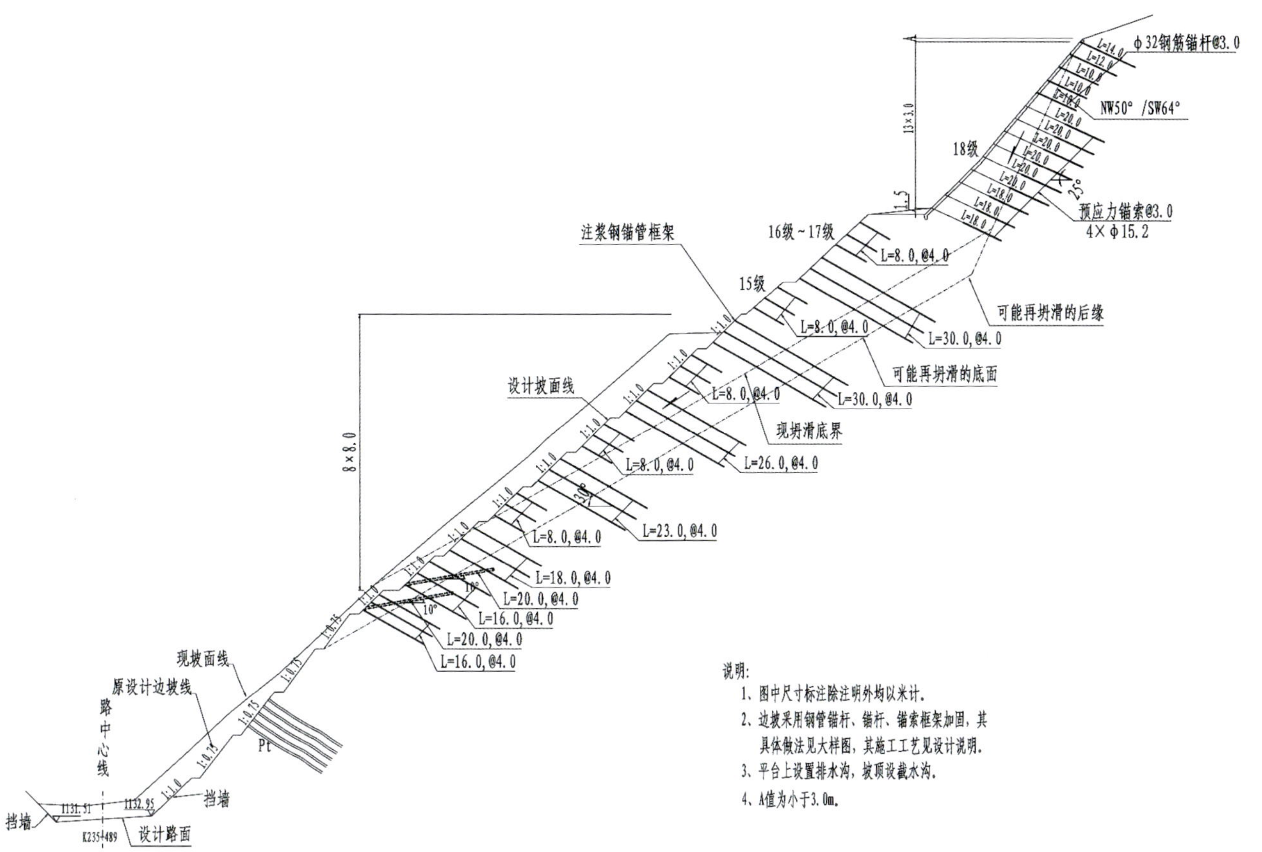

图 2.26 K235+480～+550右侧大型坍塌体治理断面图

Fig 2.26 Cross-section of treatment for the large-scale landslide to the right of K235+480~+550

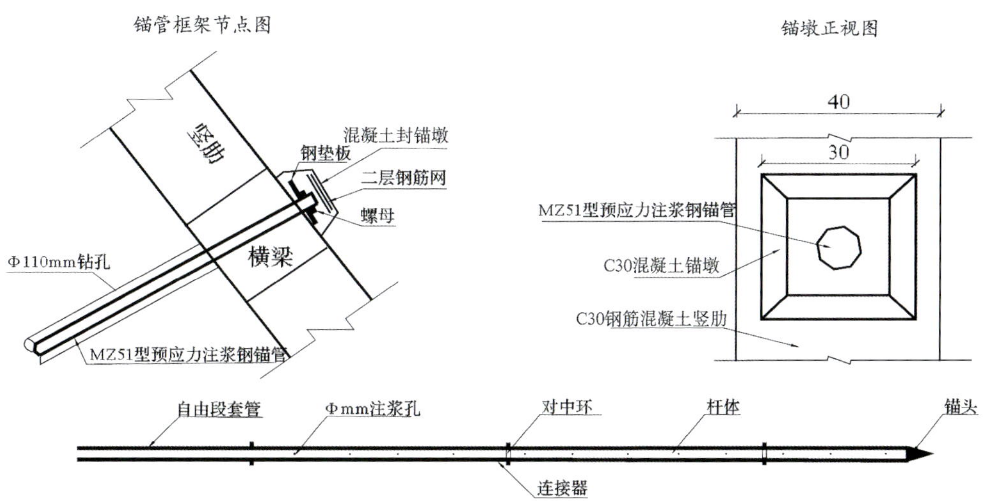

图 2.27 MZ51型预应力钢锚管结构（尺寸单位：cm）

Fig 2.27 Structure of the MZ51 prestressed steel anchor-tube

图 2.28① 治理工程施工中

Landslide treatment

图 2.28② 竣工后边坡全貌

Full view of the slope after treatment

■西（安）汉（中）高速公路沿线的边坡工程

西汉高速公路穿越横亘于中国中部的天然屏障——秦岭、巴山山地。主线全长255km，概算投资近139亿元，是中国同时期高速公路中一次性投资最大、里程最长、难度最大的建设项目，同时也是同时期中国山区高速公路的生态样板工程。

西汉高速公路穿越秦岭主山脉，山高沟深，地形、地质条件极为复杂。为有效保护沿线的结构与生态环境，采取了开挖隧道，架设桥梁，少挖、多保护、多还原等措施，最大限度地减少了公路沿线的边坡高度和高边坡数量。全线共设桥梁422座，隧道136座，山区路段桥隧比例占到近70%，其中穿越秦岭的路段几乎没有路基，桥隧工程占线路总长的76%。

■Slope project along the Xi'an-Hanzhong Highway

With a total length of 255 km, the Xi'an-Hanzhong Highway cuts through the Qin Mountain and the Bashan Mountain a natural barrier in central China. A total of RMB13.9 billion was invested in this project. It was the longest, the most difficult, and the most heavily invested highway projects built in the same period. It has also been held up as a role model for othezr highway projects in mountainous regions in China for its eco-friendly engineering.

The Xi'an-Hanzhong Highway passes through the main mountain ranges of Qin Mountain, where the terrain and geological conditions are extremely complex. In order to protect the geological structure and ecology along the highway, measures were taken to reduce slope height and the number of high slopes: tunnels were excavated, bridges were built, excavations were minimized and conservation was emphasized. A total of 136 tunnels and 422 bridges have been constructed; 70% of the highway in the mountainous region comprises bridges and tunnels. The section that cuts through Qin Mountain is almost devoid of roadbases. Tunnels and bridges account for 76% of the total length of the highway.

图2.29 隧道洞门坡面保持原始状态

Fig 2.29 The slope surface at the tunnel entrance is kept in harmony with the environment

图 2.30　沿线边坡防护大量采用了植物防护和柔性防护，同时在工程防护的基础上，对沿线部分高边坡采用客土喷播和土工格室种草等进行坡面绿化，植物种子配比采用草、灌、花相结合，落实了“对环境最小程度地破坏、最大程度地恢复”的原则。

Fig 2.30 Large amounts of vegetation and flexible preventions were used on slope surfaces. Greening on the landslide surface was achieved by planting grass, shrubs and flowers for conservation and to minimize adverse effects on the environment.

① 布鲁克柔性防护网防护隧道洞门外岩石边坡

Brook flexible protection net

② 挂网客土喷播草防护岩石路堑边坡（客土喷播施工）

Spray-planting on the slope surface

③ 挂网客土喷播草防护岩石路堑边坡（防护效果）

Effectiveness of spray-planting

④ 采用浆砌片石拱形骨架、水泥混凝土方格框架、水泥混凝土六边形砖和植生袋综合防护岩质高边坡

Protection by planting in the concrete frames for the high rock landslide

⑥ 采用锚索框架和客土喷播植草综合处治不稳定边坡

Integrated treatment of concrete frame reinforced with anchor and planting for the landslide

⑤ 六边形砖孔内栽植植生袋

Plants in bags buried in the hexagon brick frame

⑦ 采取精准的控制性光面爆破技术，保留自然山石为路基边坡，和周围景观浑然一体

Road embankment and its surroundings are integrated by precisely controlled smooth blasting

■铜（川）黄（陵）高速公路沿线的典型边坡工程

铜川至黄陵高速公路全长75km，穿越陕北黄土高原南部的黄土梁峁与低山丘陵区（北山），地形、地质条件较为复杂，工程建设中对大量的高边坡和滑坡进行了治理，成效显著。铜黄高速公路沿线黄土边坡最高达88m；风化泥岩、砂岩、碳质泥岩互层的边坡118段，最高达76m；治理各类滑坡28处，累计长达7.4km。高边坡和滑坡病害处治采用的主要措施包括：削方减载、锚索框架梁、锚索抗滑桩、预应力锚杆、普通抗滑桩、仰斜排水孔、挂网喷浆、柔性防护网、浆砌防护、植被防护等。

■Typical Slope Projects along the Tongchuan-Huangling Expressway

Total length of the Tongchuan-Huangling Expressway is 75 km. It crosses over loess ridge and hilly regions on the south of the loess plateau in the north of Shaanxi Province. Topographies and geologic conditions are relatively complex. Plenty of high slopes and landslides have been treated during the expressway construction. The maximum height of slopes along the Tongchuan-Huangling Expressway is 88 m. There are 118 slopes with interbeddings of weathered mudstone, sandstone and carbonaceous mudstone and the maximum height is 76 m. Totally 28 different landslides have been treated and the cumulative length is 7.4 km. Main treatment measures for high slopes and landslides include: slope cutting and deloading, anchor-framework beam, anchorage anti-slide pile, prestressed anchor, anti-slide pile, drainage hole, reinforcement mat and spray concrete, flexible protective net, wet masonry protection and vegetative protection, etc.

西河水库滑坡治理工程

西河水库滑坡为一巨型基岩古滑坡，由于路堑的开挖，引起古滑坡复活（1999年3月），形成新的滑坡，属岩质牵引式逆层滑坡。铜黄高速公路从滑坡的中前部通过。滑坡治理以“削头、固腰、强脚”为治理理念，采用锚索框架梁和抗滑桩、挡土墙联合支护综合治理滑坡，并完善坡体排水措施。

The Project for the Xihe Reservoir Landslide Treatment

The Xihe Reservoir Landslide is an ancient huge bedrock landslide. Excavations induced revival of a fossil landslide (March. 1999) and a new landslide arose. The Tongchuan-Huangling Expressway passes the middle-fore part of the landslide. Based on the ideas of “cutting head, fixing middle, reinforcing toe”, various approaches including reinforced framework beams with anchoring and slope stabilizing piles, retaining walls are used. Drainage measures were provided.

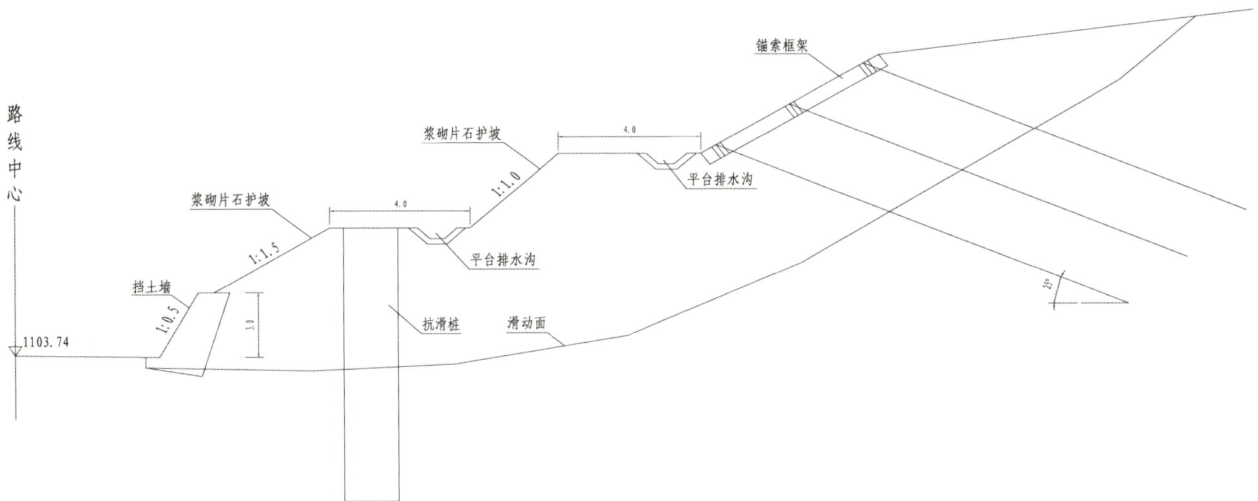

图 2.31　典型横断面方案设计图（尺寸单位：m）

Fig 2.31　A typical cross section of the Xihe Reservoir landslide treatment project

图 2.32　西河水库滑坡治理工程全貌
Fig 2.32 General view of the treatment project for the Xihe Reservoir Landslide

图 2.33　坡脚抗滑挡墙和锚索框架梁

锚索框架采用 C30 钢筋混凝土，梁宽 100cm，厚 80cm。框架节点间距 3m，每个节点设置一束由 9 根预应力钢绞线组成的锚索，长度 31～37m，单束锚索张拉应力为 1000kN。

Fig 2.33 A retaining wall and reinforced framework beams with anchoring are built at the slope toe

The concrete framework beams are placed with C30 reinforced with anchors. Widths of the anchorage framework beams are 1000 mm and their thicknesses are 800 mm. Spaces of framework nodes are 3 m. At each node, an anchor of nine prestressed steel wires is set. Their lengths are 31~37 m and the tension force is 1000 kN for each anchor.

图 2.34 路基边坡平台截水沟与抗滑桩

抗滑桩采用悬臂式，桩长 17.8～21m 之间，嵌入稳定基岩 8m。桩间距 8～10m，桩截面 3(3.5)m × 2(2.5)m。

Fig2.34 Intercepting drains and slope stabilizing piles on slope platforms of the subgrade

The slope stabilizing piles are cantilever piles. They are 17.8~21 m long and embeded into the stable bedrock 8 m long. Spaces between two piles are 8~10 m and cross section areas of piles are 3(3.5) m × 2(2.5) m.

■廓家河滑坡治理工程

廓家河滑坡为一巨型牵引式黄土滑坡，由于公路路堑的开挖，使古滑坡复活。采用预应力高强锚索抗滑桩和预应力锚杆联合支护体系等措施进行治理防护。

(1) 预应力高强锚索抗滑桩。桩间距 6m，桩长为 16～25m，桩径为 2m × 3m。在距桩顶 2.2m 左右范围分别设置倾角为 35°、45° 两根 OVM 15-19 型预应力锚索。锚索由 19 根直径 15.24mm 钢绞线组成一束，长度为 16～26m，其锚固深度不小于 8m。单束锚索张拉应力均为 2100kN。

(2) 预应力锚杆：用于加固锚索桩上部不稳定边坡块体。锚孔间距均为 2.5m。锚杆采用直径 28mm Ⅱ 级螺纹钢筋，锚杆孔深为 18～21.5m，锚杆俯角 25°，锚固段长度 6m，设计张拉力 200kN。

（资料来源：史彦文）

■ The Treatment Project for the Kuojiahe Landslide

The Kuojiahe Landslide is a huge revived ancient landslide induced by road excavation. The treatment project was performed by using the combination retaining structures of pre-stressed anchorage slope stabilizing piles and pre-stressed anchor bolts.

(1) Prestressed anchorage anti-slide piles: Spaces of piles are 6 m. Piles are 16 ~25 m long and their diameters are 2~3 m. Two OVM 15~19 prestressed anchors are setup on the both sides of the top for each pile. The anchors compose of 19 prestressed steel wires with diameter of 15.24 mm and lengths of 18~24 m. Their anchorage depths are not less than 8 m and tension force of each anchor is 2100 kN.

(2) Prestressed anchor bolts: They are constructed to reinforce the unstable slope blocks on the upper part of anchorage piles. Their spaces are 2.5 m. The anchor blots are made of screwed reinforcement with 28 mm diameter. Depths of anchor holes are 18 ~ 21.5 m. Depression angles of anchor bolts are 25° and lengths of anchorage segment are 6 m. Their design tension forces are 200 kN. (SHI Yanwen)

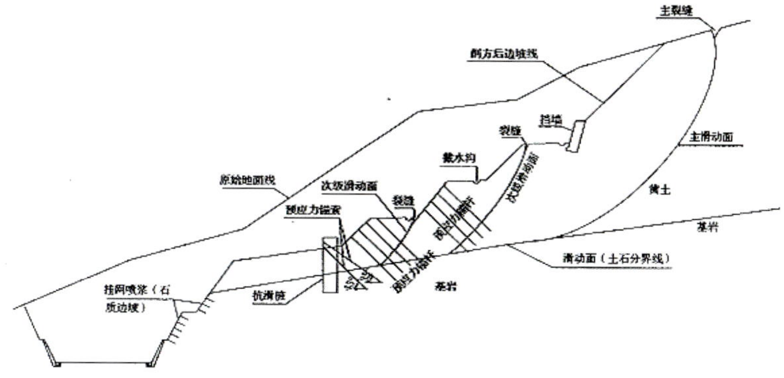

图 2.35　滑坡治理工程典型横断面图

Fig2.35 A typical cross section of the landslide treatment project

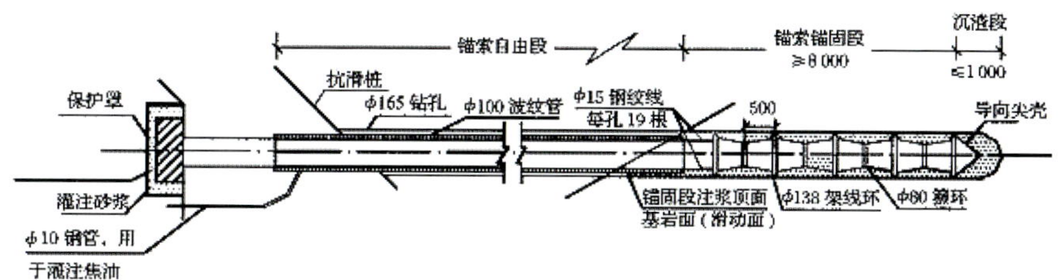

图2.36　预应力高强锚索抗滑桩锚索结构图(尺寸单位:mm)

Fig2.36 A diagram of prestressed anchorage slope stabilizing piles

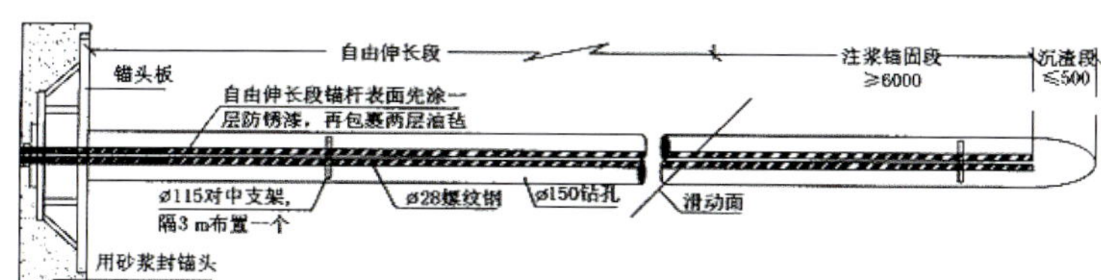

图 2.37　预应力锚杆结构图（尺寸单位:mm)

Fig2.37 A diagram of prestressed anchor bolts

图 2.38　采用锚索框架、锚墩、主动防护网等综合防护加固的岩石高边坡

Fig2.38 The high rock slope protected by reinforced frameworks and piers with anchoring and active protective net

第Ⅲ章 中国黄土高原地区的公路工程边坡

Chapter Ⅲ Highway Engineered Slopes in Loess Plateau Regions

■黄土是一种具有特殊性质的第四纪松散沉积物，中国黄土和黄土状土的分布面积为 64 × 10^4 km^2，广泛分布于北纬 34° ～45° 之间的干旱和半干旱区内，其中以秦岭以北、长城以南、太行山以西、日月山以东的黄土高原分布最为集中，黄土沉积最为典型。由于黄土结构疏松、垂直节理发育以及地表植被稀疏、暴雨集中等原因，导致黄土高原地区的土壤侵蚀极为严重，形成了沟壑纵横、支离破碎的地形地貌景观。

■Loess is a kind of loose Quaternary deposit with special properties. The area of loess or loess-like soil in China is about 64× 10^4 km^2, spawning the arid and semi-arid area between north latitude 34° to 45°. The highest concentration of loess plateau and the most typical sedimentation are located north of the Qin Mountain, south of the Great Wall, west of the Tai Hang Mountain and east of the Riyue Mountain. Because of the loose soil composition, vertical structural joints, vegetation rarefaction and high intensity of rainstorm, soil erosion has become an extremely serious problem in the loess plateau, resulting in a fragmented relief and topography typified by deep crisscrossed gullies.

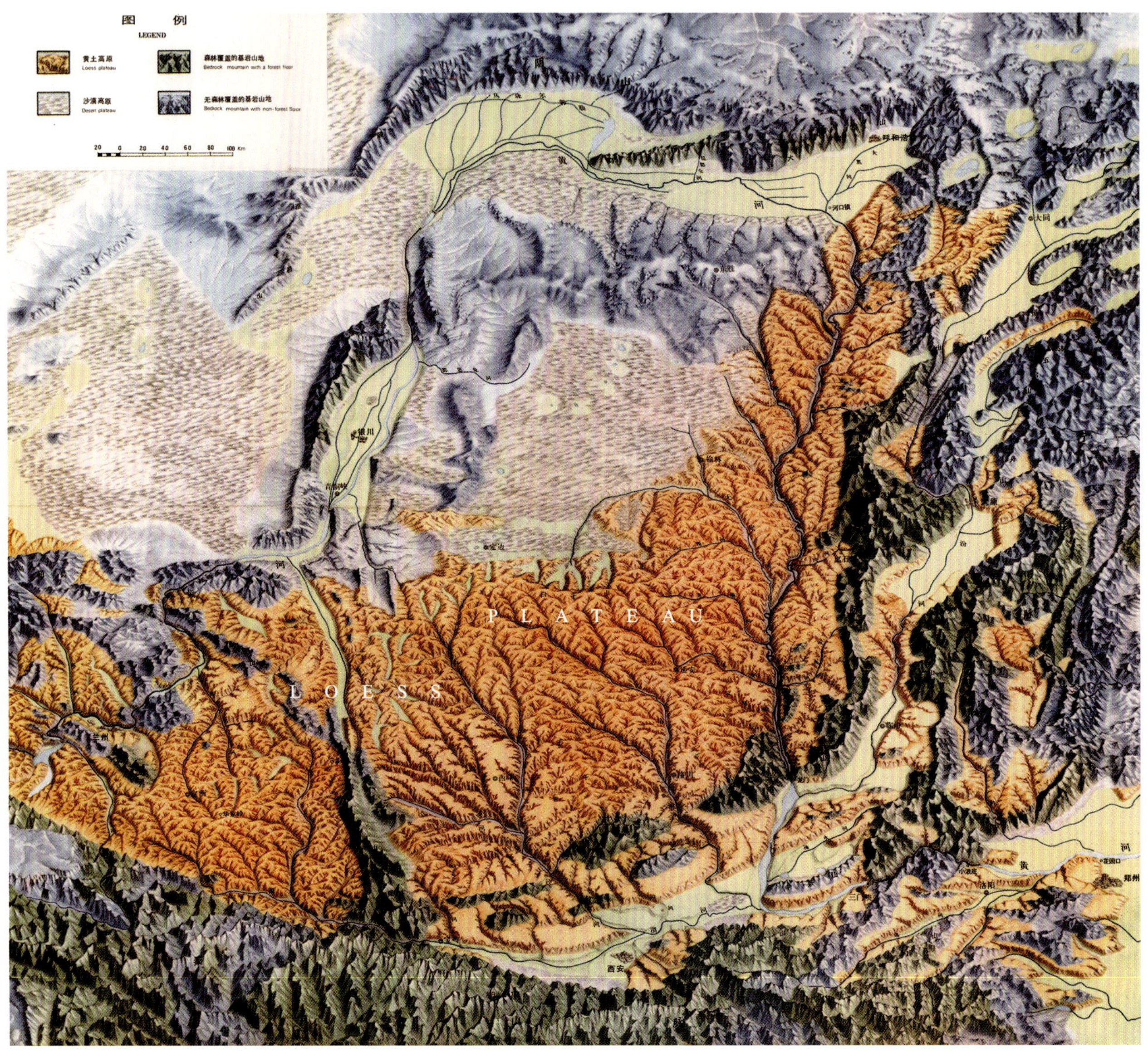

图 3.1 黄河中游黄土分布图

资料来源：《黄河中游区域工程地质》（地质出版社，1986）

Fig 3.1 Distribution of loess along the midstream of the Yellow River

Document resource: 'Engineering geology along the midstream of the Yellow River'(Geology Press, 1986)

■20世纪90年代中后期，中国开始在黄土高原地区大量兴建高等级公路。典型工程项目主要有：甘肃柳（沟河）忠（和）高速公路、白（银）兰（州）高速公路、陕西黄（陵）延（安）高速公路、吴（堡）子（洲）高速公路、河南郑（州）洛（阳）高速公路、山西运（城）三（门峡）高速公路等。这些作为带状工程的高速公路穿越沟壑密布、地形崎岖的黄土区，路线方案虽经反复优化后，仍不可避免地要进行大量开挖或填筑，形成众多的深路堑、高路堤。

■A large number of expressways have been built in China's loess plateau regions since the mid to late 1990s, typical examples being the Liugouhe-Zhonghe expressway in Gansu province, Baiyin-Lanzhou expressway, Huangling-Yan'an expressway in Shaanxi Province, Zhengzhou-Luoyang expressway in Henan Province, and Yuncheng-Sanmenxia expressway in Shanxi Province. As these expressways wind along the loess plateau region, despite repeated refinement of the route plans, a lot of deep cuttings and high embankments by excavation or fill are still required.

图3.2① 穿越陇西黄土高原的柳沟河至忠河高速公路

Expressways and slopes in the loess plateau region

图3.2② 纵穿陕北黄土高原的黄陵至延安高速公路

Huangling-Yan'an expressway

图 3.2③ 横贯陕北黄土高原的吴堡子至子洲高速公路

Wubo-Zizhou Expressway

■黄土边坡坡度过缓或坡长过长时，坡面径流冲刷将大大加剧。因此，为了既能保证黄土边坡稳定，又能防止边坡侵蚀破坏，高等级公路上的黄土路堑边坡通常采用阶梯形。单级坡高 8～12m，单级坡率 1∶0.5～1∶1.5，小平台宽 2～3m，大平台宽 4～6m。当边坡高度超过 30m 时，常在边坡中部设置 1～2 级宽度为 10～20m 的减载平台。

依据边坡坡率和平台宽度的不同组合，阶梯形边坡分为陡坡率窄平台、陡坡率宽平台、缓坡率窄平台和缓坡率宽平台等几种类型。

■Scouring by the stream on the slope surface may be amplified when the slope angle is too low or the length of slope surface is too long. So the slopes bordering the expressways in the loess plateau regions are usually terraced to ensure slope stability and prevention soil erosion. The height of each single step ranges from 8 m to 12 m and the slope ratio ranges from 1:0.5 to 1:1.5. The widths of the berms range from 2 m to 3 m for small ones and 4 m to 6 m for large ones. When the height of the slope is higher than 30 m, one or two berms with widths of 10m to 20 m are built in the middle of the slope to reduce the loading.

According to the different combination of slope angles and berm widths, terraced slopes can be divided into several types: steep slope with narrow berm, steep slope with wide berm, gentle slope with narrow berm, gentle slope with wide berm.

图 3.3 西安绕城高速公路、机场高速公路、西安至阎良高速公路上的缓坡率宽平台型黄土边坡。分级高度 5m 左右，坡率缓于 1∶1，平台宽度大于 4m，边坡总高度小于 15m。低缓边坡路堑宽敞，坡面容易种植绿化。(焦臣 摄)

Fig 3.3 Gentle slopes with wide berms along the Xi'an city ring expressway, airport expressway, and Xi'an-Yanliang expressway. The height of each single step is about 5 m, slope ratio is less than 1:1, berm width is larger than 4 m and total height of slope is smaller than 15 m. This kind of slope is easy for greening. (JIAO Chen)

① 枣树沟路段（第Ⅰ~Ⅱ级坡面出露砾石层）：窄平台阶梯形，边坡高度68m。

Expressway at Zaoshugou Road(Gravel appear on the surface of the first and second step of the slope):Terraced slope with narrow berms and a total height of 68 m.

② 大庙路段（边坡底部有掏沙采空区）：宽平台阶梯形，边坡高度大于70m。

Expressway at Damiao(with excavation damaged zone at the toe of slope):Terraced slope with wide berms; Height of slope is greater than 70 m.

图3.4　柳忠高速公路沿线大于30的黄土高边坡20余处。坡体土质以Q_3风积或冲积黄土为主。边坡采用下陡上缓的阶梯形，分级坡高10m，分级坡率1∶0.5~1∶1.0，平台宽2m或5m。（鲁安新　摄）

Fig 3.4 There are more than 20 loess slopes with a slope angle larger than 30 degree along the Liugouhe-Zhonghe expressway. Slope soil is mainly composed of aeolian or alluvial loess in Q_3. Slope ratio near the toe is smaller than at the top. Each step is 10 m high; slope ratio ranges from 1:0.5 to 1:1.0; berm width is either 2 m or 5 m.(LU Anxin)

图 3.5 黄延高速公路沿线开挖深度超过 30m 的路堑 30 余处，最大削坡高度 80m。坡体土质上部以 Q_3 风积黄土为主，下部以 Q_2 黄土为主。广泛采用了“低坡高、陡坡率、宽平台”的高边坡形式。坡高 8m，坡率 1∶0.5，平台宽 4～7m，大平台宽 10～18m。（韩文宪 提供）

Fig 3.5 There are more than 30 cuttings with a height of more than 30 m along the Huangling-Yan'an expressway, and the highest one is about 80 m. Slope soil is mainly composed of aeolian loess in Q_3 in the upper part, and loess in Q_2 in the lower part. A widely adopted slope form is one with lower slopes, large slope ratios and wide berms. Slope height is 8 m, slope ratio is 1:0.5 and berm width is 4~7 m (10~18 m for larger berms).(HAN Wenxian)

■为利用挖余土方、减少占地，常在不宜修建桥梁的黄土冲沟路段填筑黄土高路堤。路堤边坡视填筑高度采用折线形或阶梯形，分级坡高 8～12m，坡率 1∶1.5～1∶2.0。为减少工后差异沉降，高路堤填筑时需提高分层压实度，或采取强夯、冲击碾压等措施进行压密处理。

■In order to reuse the loess soil after excavation, it is usually used to build loess embankments in some deeply cut sections where bridges are not suitable. The slope of the embankment can be either polygonal or terraced depending on the height of the fill. The height of each step is about 8 m to12 m and the slope ratio is about 1:1.5~1:2.0. In order to reduce uneven settlement after construction, the soil should be densified by compaction or compaction by vibrating roller.

图3.6 柳忠高速公路沿线填筑高度大于20m的黄土高路堤10余处，边坡最大高度38.5m。边坡坡率：堤顶以下8m以内为1∶1.5；8～20m为1∶1.75；20m处设2m宽平台，20m以下为1∶2.0。坡面采用浆砌片石拱形骨架或预制混凝土方格防护。（赵永国 摄）

Fig 3.6 There are more than 10 loess slopes with a height greater than 20 m along the Liuguohe-Zhongkou expressway, with the highest one about 38.5 m. Taking the top of a slope as a datum, within the region from the top to 8 m below the datum, the slope ratio is about 1:1.5; from 8 m to 20 m below the datum, the ratio is 1:1.75. At 20 m below the datum, a 2 m wide berm is built. Below 20 m, the slope ratio is about 1:2.0. An arching frame of grouted stone pitching or precast concrete segment is used to protect the slope surface.(ZHAO Yongguo)

■由于黄土高边坡的坡面面积较大，为减少工程量，早期的黄土边坡坡面一般以土质裸坡为主，或仅对边坡平台、坡脚部位进行防护，坡面易发生坡面剥落、冲刷等病害，且景观效果较差。

■ As loess slopes have large surface area, to cut down on engineering work, earlier slopes were generally left without any treatment or only the berms and slope toes were protected. As a result, the slope surfaces are prone to exfoliation and soil erosion which render them unsightly.

① 裸露黄土边坡坡面剥落、冲刷 *Local collapse at the toe of slope*

② 坡脚土体过湿导致局部坍塌

Exfoliation of naked loess slopes

图 3.7　黄土路堑边坡的侵蚀主要表现为坡面剥落、冲刷和坡体坍塌、滑坡等，黄土的湿陷性和弱抗冲性是边坡产生病害的主要原因。(倪万魁 提供)

Fig 3.7 Erosion of loess slope mostly takes the form of exfoliation, surface erosion, collapse, landslide, etc. which are mainly caused by the collapsibility and weak impact resistance of loess.(NI Wankui)

■水的侵蚀是诱发黄土边坡变形失稳的主要原因，因此黄土边坡防护首先必须做好坡面和坡体的排水。坡面排水系统由坡顶截水沟、平台排水沟、边沟、急流槽等组成，主要是防治边坡坡面冲刷；坡体排水主要是防治边坡整体失稳，常采用仰斜排水孔、盲沟。

■Erosion by water is the main reason for deformation and instability of the loess slope, so drainage on the slope surface and inside the slope is a priority. The drainage system on the slope surface consists of intercepting ditches at the slope top, drainage ditches on the berms, side ditches, chutes and so on, mainly to avoid erosion on the surface. Drain holes and blind ditches are mainly used to sustain the stability of the slope.

①

图 3.8 白（银）兰（州）高速公路隧道洞门黄土高边坡坡顶截水沟（鲁安新 摄）

Fig 3.8 Intercepting ditch at the top of slope near the tunnel portal of Baiyin-Lanzhou expressway(Lu Anxin)

■进入21世纪以来，黄土工程边坡建设中开始注重采取植被技术，如土工网植草、穴播、平台植树等。这些措施既能保护坡面，又达到了绿化边坡、美化环境的目的，使生态得以快速恢复。

■Planting protection methods have received more attention since the beginning of the 21st- century, such as geotextile nets with composite vegetation, cavern-planting, planting on berms and so on.

图 3.9 黄（陵）延（安）高速公路、吴（堡）子（洲）高速公路等应用植物穴播技术防护黄土边坡（韩文宪 提供）

Fig 3.9 Planting protection method by cavern-planting in Huangling-Yan'an (Wu bao-Zizhou Expressway et.al)(HAN Wenxian)

① 坡面钻孔（45° 斜孔）

Hole on the slope surface(with an inclination of 45°)

② 孔内填埋肥料、草种

Embed seeds and fertilizer in the hole

③ 浇水育苗后种子发芽(约5天后)
Germination after watering(About 5 days later)

④ 幼苗展叶（浇水约15天后）
Germination(About 15 days later)

⑤ 坡面植被逐步形成
Development of planting protection

⑥ 综合防护效果
Comprehensive protection effects

图 3.10　黄延高速公路采用挂网客土喷播植草防护黄土路堑边坡（韩文宪 提供）
Fig 3.10　Protection by spraying glass-seeds with net on loess slope along the Huangling-Yan'an expressway(HAN Wenxian)

① 坡面清理后挂网
Suspended-net afer clearance on the slope surface

② 选择当地适生草种
Choose appropriate seeds

③ 现场配制用于喷播的客土基质 *Basical material made on site for spraying*

④ 喷播后采用无纺布人工养护 *Artificial maintenance by non-woven material after spraying*

⑤ 幼苗茁壮成长，草被逐步形成
Gradual formation of protection layer with growth of seedlings

⑥ 综合防护效果
Comprehenisve protection results

图 3.11 绛帐－法门寺－汤峪二级公路
Fig 3.11 In the Jiangzhang-Famensi-Tangyu class II highway

① 防护前
Before protection

② 防护后
After protection

图 3.12 在黄土边坡平台上栽植乔灌树木可达到防护边坡和美化路容的双重目的。(倪万魁 提供)
Fig 3.12 Protection and beautification by planting on berms of loess slopes .(NI Wankui)

■在坡面上砌筑浆砌片石骨架或混凝土框架，然后在骨架内采用人工种植或机械喷播的方式种植草皮或灌木，可达到加固与防护兼顾、刚柔相济的效果。

■After building frames of grouted rubble or of concrete on the surface of the slope, both artificial planting and spraying planting by machine were adopted to plant greensward or shrubs.

图3.13 铜黄高速公路采用浆砌片石拱形骨架植草防护黄土路堑高边坡。(倪万魁 提供)

Fig 3.13 Protection method using arching frames of rubble masonry with planting on the Tong- Huang expressway.(NI Wankui)

图 3.14 黄延高速公路采用浆砌片石骨架+预制混凝土空心砖+植被综合防护隧道洞门黄土高边坡（侯军亭 提供）

Fig 3.14 Comprehensive protection of loess slope near tunnel portal was adopted using frames of rubble masonry, precast concrete hollow blocks and planting on the Huangling-Yan'an expressway(HOU Junting)

① 骨架、喷播施工（鲁安新 摄） *Frame and spraying(LU Anxin)*

② 防护效果（朱聪功 摄） *After treatment(ZHU Conggong)*

图 3.15 兰州东出口道路黄土高边坡的综合防护

第Ⅰ级采用浆砌片石护面墙防护，第Ⅱ～Ⅳ（Ⅴ）级采用混凝土方格骨架加植被防护，以上各级采用液力喷播植草防护。

Fig 3.15 Comprehensive protection of high loess slope at the east exit at Lanzhou

The first step was treated by grouted rubble facing walls, and the second to fourth steps were treated by hollow concrete frames. Planting protection is also included in the whole treatment.

第Ⅳ章 中国寒区的公路与铁路工程边坡

Chapter Ⅳ Highway & Railway Engineered Slopes in Frozen Ground Regions

■寒区占据了中国约75%的国土面积，其中多年冻土区和季节冻土区的面积分别占21.5%和53.5%。中国的寒区主要分布在长江以北的广大地区，并以青藏高原的低纬度高原多年冻土、东北大小兴安岭地区的高纬度多年冻土和东北中南部地区的中－深季节冻土为突出代表。

冻土是一种温度强敏感土体，温度的正负变化可使土体中水分迁移和发生相变，引发冻土一系列复杂的力学行为变化，这一过程可导致土体在强度和变形方面发生质的变化，并直接影响到以冻土为载体的工程边坡的稳定性，使寒区道路工程边坡产生滑塌等病害。

中国多年冻土地区公路、铁路工程相对较少，但这些工程对于区域社会、经济发展具有十分重要的意义。如青藏高原的青藏公路（109国道）、青康公路（214国道）、新藏公路（219国道）以及青藏铁路等，东北高纬度多年冻土区的黑北公路以及大小兴安岭林区的公路和铁路等。

■Frozen soil regions in China occupies about 75% of the land area of the country, of which permafrost and seasonally frozen soil areas account for 21.5% and 53.5% respectively. Most of them are located on the north of the Yangtze River. Typical frozen soils in China include the permafrost soils on the Qinghai-Tibet Plateau at low latitudes and on the Khingan Mountains in the northeast of China at high latitudes, and the intermediate-deep seasonally frozen soils in the south-central part of northeastern regions.

Frozen soil is a temperature-sensitive soil .Both positive and negative changes in temperature can produce moisture migration and phase changes in the soil, leading to a series of complex changes in mechanical behaviour. This process can result in significant changes in soil strength and deformation characteristics and then produce a direct impact on slope stability in frozen soils, causing some geohazards such as landside in engineered slopes in the frozen soil regions.

There are relatively few road projects in the permafrost regions of China. However, these projects are of great significance for regional social and economic development. The important projects include the Qinghai-Tibet Highway (National Highway No. 109), the Qing-Kang Highway (National Highway No. 214), the Xinjiang-Tibet Highway (National Highway No. 219), the Qinghai-Tibet Railway, the Hei-Bei Highway in the northeastern permafrost areas at high latitudes, and highways and railways on the Khingan Mountains.

图 4.1 中国冻土及冻土区主要公路、铁路工程分布图

Fig 4.1 The map of permafrost and higway & railway engineering projects distribution in china

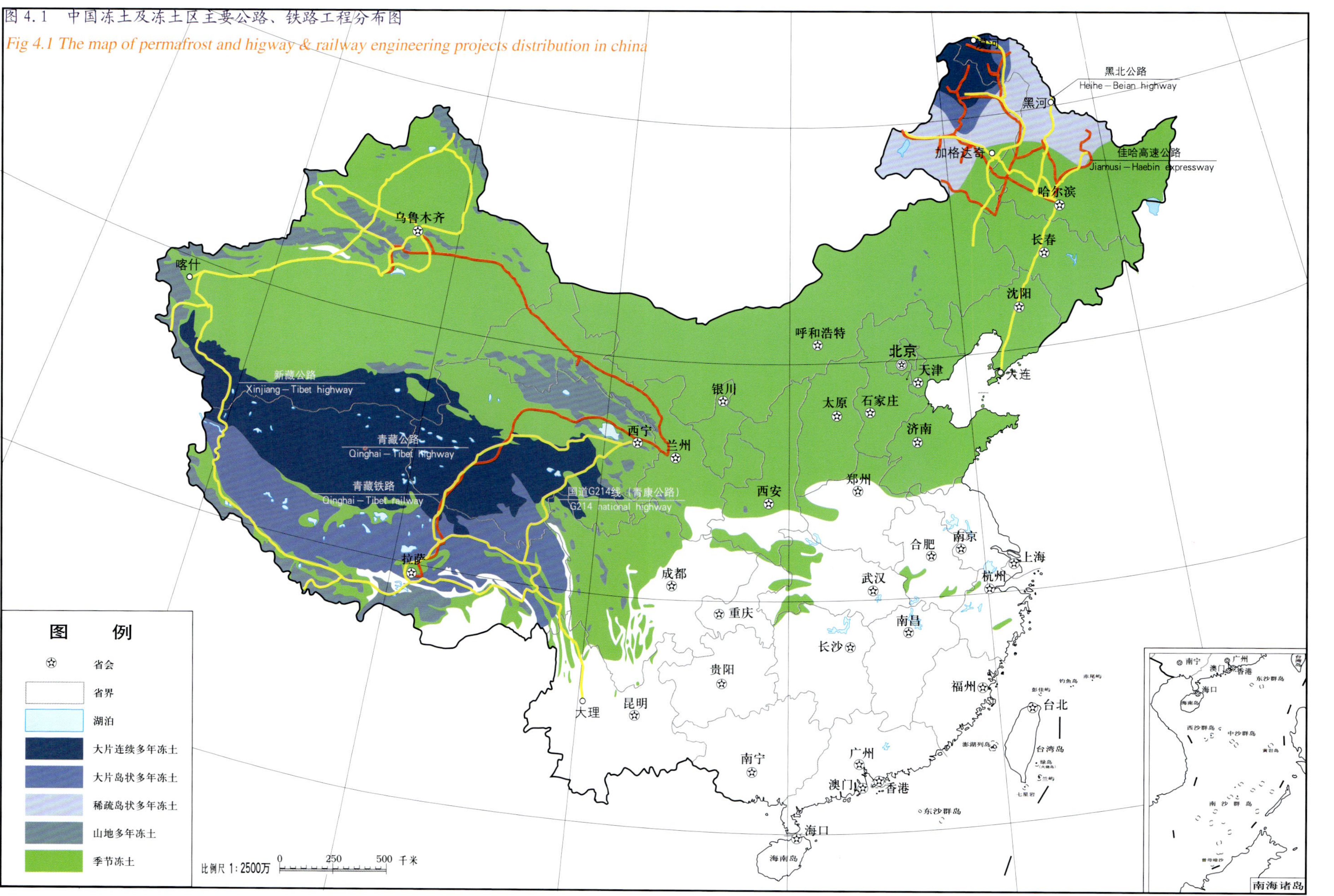

■青藏高原多年冻土区是世界上中、低纬度地带海拔最高、面积最大的多年冻土区，冻土分布面积约149 × 10^4平方公里，约占中国多年冻土面积的70%，高原多年冻土分布区域海拔一般均超过4500m。

近年来随着青藏公路维修与改建及青藏铁路的建设，冻土区斜坡稳定性问题日益受到重视。高原冻土区筑路工程中，开挖或扰动了高含冰量的冻土斜坡时，经常会出现热融导致的滑塌病害。多年冻土区的道路工程建设中首先尽量避免多年冻土的开挖和扰动。在不可避免的开挖地区，路堑边坡一般采用换填处理，并在坡面设置保护措施，坡顶和坡脚设置防、排水工程。路堤边坡处理则本着保护冻土的原则，结合支挡结构采用主动减少土体吸热、消散土体热能的工程措施，冷却坡体土体使其保持冻结状态，如碎石覆盖、移植草皮护坡、设置热管等，或有选择性地采用隔热材料覆盖，但各种措施中均注重设置良好的隔水、排水措施。

■ Among the permafrost regions at intermediate-low latitudes in the world, the regions on the Qinghai-Tibet Plateau are the highest and largest. These regions have an area of 1,490,000 km^2, which is about 70 % of the area of permafrost regions in China. The elevation of permafrost regions on plateaus is generally over 4,500 m.

In recent years, with the maintenance and alterations of the Qinghai-Tibet Highway and the construction of the Qinghai-Tibet Railway, the problems on slope stability in frozen soils have received increasing attention. During road construction in frozen soils on plateaus, excavation or disturbance of frozen soil slopes that have high ice contents often leads to thaw slumping. Therefore, it is a primary issue to try avoiding any excavation and disturbance of permafrost soils during road construction in these soils. In the area where excavation is inevitable, replacement methods are generally used for cut slopes. In addition, protection measures are set up on slope surfaces, and waterproofing and drainage works are adopted at the crest and toe of the slopes. In order to protect frozen soils in cut slopes, some engineering measures are used in retaining structures to actively reduce heat absorption by soils and dissipate heat in soils. These measures are expected to cool slopes and keep soils frozen. The engineering measures include crushed gravel pavement, greensward transplant, installation of thermosyphons and coverage by thermal-insulation materials. All of the measures incorporate as a rule high performance waterproofing and drainage installations.

图 4.2　路堑边坡开挖引起的热融滑塌。公路施工开挖后斜坡产生的热融滑塌和大量融化水（路面被覆盖、浸泡）。（据吴紫汪）

Fig4.2 Thaw slumping was caused by excavation of the slope toe. Thaw slumping occurred and melted water seeped out soon after the excavation during highway construction (the highway was buried and softened as a result). (WU Ziwang)

图 4.3 未采取坡体特殊加固的路堑边坡，在施工完成后不久即出现坡顶开裂、坡面隆起和开裂以及坡脚积水软化。坡面混凝土骨架及小型L挡墙无法抗拒土体变形压力即遭破坏。

Fig 4.3 A cut and filled slope without any special reinforcements in permafrost regions in the Qinghai-Tibet Plateau. The slope deformed soon after construction. This led to cracks on the top, heave and cracks on the surface and the slope was softened by water gathered on the toe. The concrete framework and small L-type concrete blocks on the slope surface were damaged by slope deformation.

① 坡脚积水（冰）

Water seepage on the slope toe(show as ice)

② 堑顶土体开裂
Cracks at the top of the slope

③ 阶梯状小型L挡墙的挤出和沉陷
Extrusion and settlement of small L-type retaining wall

④ 坡面混凝土骨架遭破坏
The concrete framework was damaged

图 4.4 采用一定厚度和宽度的草包袋覆盖处理热融滑塌后缘，可有效防止斜坡发生进一步滑塌。(吴紫汪)

Fig 4.4 Headwall area of a thaw slumping was covered by sandbags.(WU Ziwang)

图 4.5 2002 年修筑的路堑边坡，坡高 30m，开挖后进行坡体换填。坡面采用水泥混凝土菱形骨架护坡防护。

Fig 4.5 A cut slope with a height of 30 m was constructed in 2002. The slope soils were refilled and the surface was covered by concrete framework.

图 4.6　2002 年修筑的路堑边坡，坡高 30m，坡体采用 L 型水泥混凝土挡土墙支撑，坡面采用移植草皮、泡沫玻璃板护坡防护。

Fig 4.6 A cut slope with a height of 30 m was constructed in 2002. The slope soils were refilled and supported with L-type sheet piles. The slope surface was covered by green-sward and glass-foam insulation layer.

图 4.7　2002 年修筑的路堑边坡，坡高 20m，坡体采用小型 L 型水泥混凝土预制块阶梯状加固。

Fig 4.7 A cut slope with a height of 20 m was constructed in 2002. The slope soils were refilled and supported with small L-type concrete blocks.

图4.8 采用热管冷却坡体、路堑底部土工材料加固、坡脚排水和坡顶设置土工布隔水层和排水沟重新处理后的路堑边坡。

Fig 4.8 The cut slopes were cooled with thermosyphons. The foot part of the slopes was reinforced with geo-textile material. Drainage grooves at the toe and top of slope were constructed. The top surface was also covered by waterproof geofabric.

① 坡顶排水沟（阻隔地表水到达坡顶填土范围）

Drainage groove on the top (avoid water reaching the slope)

② 开挖排水沟暴露的厚层地下冰

Massive ground-ice exposed by top area of groove cutting

③ 路堑底部铺设保温材料

Bottom of the cutting was recovered with thermal-insulation material

④ 坡顶铺设隔水土工布

Top surface of the slope was recovered with waterproof geofabric

⑤ 坡脚设置的热管

Thermosyphone installed at the toe of the slope

⑥ 坡顶设置的热管

Thermosyphone installed at the top of the slope

⑦ 处理结束后的路堑边坡

The cut slopes after constructed

图 4.9　采用骨架护坡的路堤边坡。　*Fig 4.9　A concrete-frame reinforced embankment slope.*

图 4.10　采用碎石护坡的路堤边坡（维护路基下多年冻土，同时保护了边坡）。

Fig 4.10　A crushed gravel covered embankment slope (the gravel layer was stacked to prevent the underlying permafrost from thawing, and it stabilized the slope too).

图 4.11 路堤边坡采用的植物防护。植被护坡有利于保护多年冻土，保持边坡稳定，又与沿线环境相协调，是一项较好的防护措施。

Fig 4.11 Plant protection on embankment slopes. This treatment can stabilize the slope as well as decrease the ground temperature. It is an environment friendly protection method.

① 青藏铁路路堤边坡采用的草皮护坡（据新华网）

An embankment slope covered with greensward on the Qinghai-Tibet Railway(Xinhua Net.)

② 青藏公路路堤边坡采用的土工网植草防护（据陈建兵）

An embankment slope protected with geonet grassing on the Qinghai-Tibet Highway(CHEN Jianbing)

■佳（木斯）哈（尔滨）高速公路穿越东北中～深季节冻土区。路基边坡的冻融破坏是这一地区特殊气候条件下特有的边坡病害之一，对于有层间水发育的边坡，若只按一般圬工防护和植物防护处理，即使坡率缓至 1∶1.5～1∶1.6（约32°左右），边坡也常发生滑塌。冻融滑塌的主要表现形式一般为距坡面 10～120cm 深度范围内的浅层滑塌，并且多集中于 20～70cm 之间。

实践表明，在季节冻土区，对于存在层间水的土质路堑边坡不宜采用大幅度减缓坡率的方法来保证边坡的稳定，最关键的是要排除边坡土体中蓄积的水分。佳哈高速公路采取的抗冻融滑塌的技术措施为：采用土工滤排水材料进行边坡浅层排水，使用土工格室植草护坡，并选用根系发达、入土较深的草本植物“马蔺”（Iris ensata Thunb）作为护坡植物。这一措施综合提高了路堑边坡的浅层稳定性，取得了较好的技术经济效果。

■The Jiamusi-Harbin Highway passes through intermediate-deep seasonally frozen soil areas in the Northeastern regions. Under special climatic conditions in these areas, freeze-thaw damage in roadbed slope is one of the special slope diseases. For a slope containing much interlay water, if it is treated with only general masonry and plant protections, the slope will usually slump even if the rate of slope is reduced to 1:1.5 to 1:1.6 (about 32°). Shallow freeze-thaw slumping mainly occurs in the depths from 10 cm to 120 cm and becomes more concentrated from 20 cm to 70 cm.

Past experience shows that substantial reduction of the rate of slope should not be used to ensure slope stability for cut slopes in the seasonally frozen soils having interlayer water. The key issue is to eliminate accumulated water in the slopes. Technical measures used for preventing the Jiamusi-Harbin Highway from freeze-thaw slump include the use of geotextile filter material for drainage in shallow slope and the use of geocell grass-planting for slope protection. Iris ensata Thunb, a herb with developed root systems and a relatively large embedment depth, is selected for grass-planting. These integrated measures effectively protect cut slopes from shallow sliding, leading to good technical and economic benefits.

图 4.12 春融期间，佳哈高速公路因边坡坡面出现冻融滑塌而导致三维植被网与植物组成的防护层局部滑落。（穆万奎提供）

Fig 4.12 During the spring thawing period, a freeze-thaw slumping led to local sliding of the protective layer, which was composed of three-dimensional vegetative mesh and plants on the Jiamusi-Harbin Highway.(MU Wankui)

①排水设施完工后在坡面上展铺土工格室

A layer of geocell was installed on the slope surface after the completion of drainage facilities

②土工格室内回填客土，种植马蔺，并洒水养护

Geocells were backfilled with new soil. An Iris ensata Thunb was planted. A sprinkler system was put in place

图 4.13 佳哈高速公路采用土工滤排水材料进行边坡浅层排水，使用土工格室植草护坡。(穆万奎 提供)

Fig 4.13 In the Jiamusi-Harbin Highway project, geotextile filter materials were used for drainage in shallow slopes. A layer of geocell with grass was installed on the slope surface for slope protection. (MU Wankui)

第Ⅴ章 中国沙漠地区的公路与铁路工程边坡

Chapter Ⅴ Highway & Railway Engineered Slopes in Desert Areas

■中国是世界上沙漠分布最多的国家之一。沙漠呈一条弧形带绵延于西北、华北北部和东北西部。沙漠总面积约80多万km^2。其中西部干旱区的沙漠一般以流动沙丘为主，中北部及东北部半干旱区的沙漠一般以固定或半固定沙丘为主。

中国目前已建成沙漠公路8000多km，其中以新疆和内蒙古的沙漠公路分布最广、里程最长。

■China is one of the countries in the world with vast desert areas. These areas form an arc-shaped belt across northwest China, the northern part of north China and the western part of northeast China, with a total area of over 800,000 km^2. In general, mobile sand dunes are found in deserts in the arid area of west China, while permanent or semi-permanent sand dunes are mostly found in deserts in the semi-arid areas of north and central China and northeast China.

A total of over 8,000 km of desert highways have so far been built in China. Among them, the most widespread and the longest highways are located in the Xinjiang and Inner Mongolia Autonomous Regions.

中国沙漠地区的典型公路与铁路工程项目
Typical Highway & Railway Construction Project in Desert Areas

沙漠名称 Desert	所在省（区） Province or autonomous region	典型项目名称 Construction project
塔克拉玛干沙漠 Taklimakan Desert	新　疆 Xinjiang autonomous region	轮台至民丰公路Luntai to Minfeng highway[R1]， 阿拉尔至和田公路Alaer to Hetian highway[R2]， 塔中1井至且末公路 Tazhongyijing to Qiemo highway[R3]
腾格里沙漠 Tengger Desert	宁　夏 Ningxia autonomous region	包（头）兰（州）铁路沙坡头段 Shapotou section of Baotou to Lanzhou railway[R4]
	内蒙古 Inner Mongolia autonomous region	月亮湖旅游公路Yuelianghu tourist highway[R5]， 省道218线巴（彦浩特）吉（来泰）公路 Bayanhaoteto Jilaitai highway[R6]
库布齐沙漠 Kobq Desert	内蒙古 Inner Mongolia autonomous region	锡（尼）乌（拉山）公路 Xini to Wulashan highway[R7]
科尔沁沙地 Horqin Sands	内蒙古 Inner Mongolia autonomous region	赤（峰）通（辽）高速公路 Chifeng to Tongliao expressway[R8]
浑善达克沙地 Hunshadake Sands	内蒙古 Inner Mongolia autonomous region	国道207线锡林浩特至桑根达莱段 Xilinhaote to Sanggendalai highway[R9]， 省际通道桑根达莱至大板段 Sanggendalai to Daban highway[R10]
毛乌素沙地 Mu Us Sands	陕　西 Shaanxi Province	榆林至靖边高速公路 Yulin to Jingbian expressway[R11]， 陕蒙界高速公路 Shaanxi(Yulin) to Inner Mongolia expressway[R12]

注：表中R1～R12为典型工程项目在沙漠分布示意图中的编号。

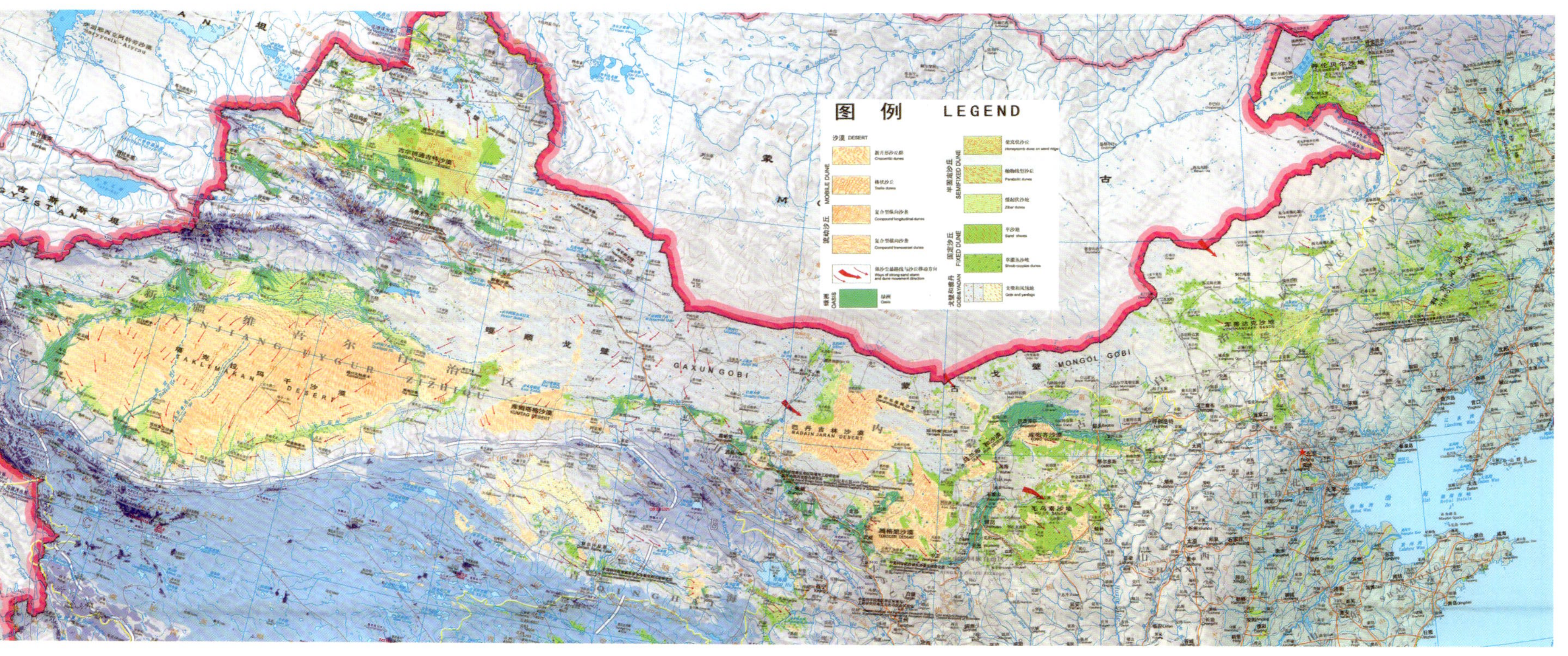

图 5.1 中国沙漠分布示意图

Fig 5.1 Schematic map of deserts in China

1 - 塔克拉玛干沙漠(Taklimakan Desert)； 2 - 古尔班通古特沙漠(Gurban Tunggut Desert);3 - 库母塔格沙漠(Kumtag Desert)；
4 - 柴达木沙漠(Caidam Desert)； 5 - 巴丹吉林沙漠(Badain Jaran Desert)； 6 - 腾格里沙漠(Tengger Desert)；
7 - 乌兰布和沙漠(Ulan Buh Desert)； 8 - 库布齐沙漠(Kobq Desert)； 9 - 毛乌素沙地(Mu Us Sands)；
10 - 浑善达克沙地(Hunshadake Sands)； 11 - 科尔沁沙地(Horqin Sands)； 12 - 呼伦贝尔沙地(Hulunbuir Sands)；
13 - 松嫩沙地(Songnen Sands)

资料来源:《中国冰川冻土沙漠图》

Date from: “MAP OF THE GLACLERS FROZER AND DESERTS IN CHINA”

■沙漠地区公路路基的典型断面：填土高度 H ≤ 1.0m 多采用坡率 1 : 3.0 ~ 1 : 10.0 的缓坡式断面；H > 1.0m 多采用坡率 1 : 3.0 ~ 1 : 8.0 的缓坡式断面或 1 : 1.5 ~ 1 : 2.0 的一般式断面；对于挖方深度 H ≤ 1.0m 的浅路堑一般采用坡率 1 : 3.0 ~ 1 : 10.0 的敞开式断面；H > 1.0m 时采用坡率 1 : 1.5 ~ 1 : 2.0 的一般式或流线型断面，并在坡脚设置 3 ~ 6m 的积沙平台。

■Typical roadbed sections of highways in desert areas: when the fill height(H) of the roadbed is less than or equal to 1.0 m, the section slope ratio (k) is equal to1:3.0~1:10.0;when H>1.0 m ,then k=1:3.0~1:8.0 or 1:1.5~1:2.0. When the excavation depth (H) of the shallow road cutting is less than or equal to 1.0 m, the cutting slope ratio (k) is equal to1:3.0~1:10.0; when H>1.0 m,k= 1:1.5~1:2.0. In this condition, a 3~6 m wide platform is also built for eolian sand deposits.

图 5.2 阿拉尔至和田沙漠公路，穿越塔克拉玛干沙漠的流沙路段。路堑边坡坡率 1 : 4，积沙平台宽度 > 3m。

Fig 5.2 A part of the Alaer-Hetian highway passes through the mobile sand in the Takimkan Desert. The slope ratio of the road cutting is 1:4 and the width of the eolian sand deposit platform is greater than 3 m.

图 5.3 内蒙省际通道桑根达莱至大板段穿越浑善达克固定沙地。路堑边坡坡率 1 : 2，积沙平台宽度 4m。

Fig 5.3 The Sanggendalai-Daban section of an inter-province highway in the Inner Mongolia Autonomous Region passes through the permanent Hunshandake Sands. The ratio of cutting slope is 1:2 and the width of the eolian sand deposit platform is 4 m.

■ 防沙工程体系：为防止风蚀和沙埋，沙漠地区的道路不仅路基主体需要防护，路基两侧一定范围也需要防护，形成系统的防沙体系。

■ Sand-protecting engineering system: to protect highways in desert areas from wind erosion and being buried by sand, apart from protecting the roadbed, both sides of the highways also need to be protected in order to form a complete sand-protecting system.

图 5.4 新疆的轮台至民丰、阿拉尔至和田、塔中至且末等沙漠公路纵贯塔克拉玛干流动沙漠，设有阻沙、固沙、输沙齐全的防沙体系，其一般结构是：路基两侧设置 30～100m 宽的固沙带，在固沙带外设 1～2 道芦苇立式栅栏。固沙带的固沙材料以芦苇方格为主，部分路段采用土工合成材料、当地棉杆和稻草等材料。（刘涛　提供）

Fig 5.4 Along the Luntai-Minfeng highway, Alaer-Hetian highway and Tazhong-Qiemo highway, which pass through the mobile sands in the Taklimakan Desert, a complete sand-protecting system has been built. It can block, bind and transfer sands. The typical structure of the system is such that on both sides of the roadbed, a sand-binding belt (30~100 m in width) is set up; next to the sand-binding belt, 1~2 standing reed fences are set up. Most of the sand-binding materials consist of reed grids; certain sections use Geo-synthetic material, local cotton bars and straw. (LIU Tao)

① 塔中至且末沙漠公路的防沙体系（在上风侧采用芦苇方格固沙，宽度 70～110m，在固沙带外的 20m 和 40m 设芦苇立式栅栏各一道；在其下风侧设芦苇方格固沙带宽 30～50m，并在固沙带外 20m 设芦苇栅栏 1 道）

Sand-protecting system along the Tazhong-Qiemo highway (On the upwind side, the reed grid belt is used to bind sand. Its width is 70~110 m. 20 m and 40 m away from the belt, two standing reed fences are set up. On the downwind side, the reed grid sand barrier belt 30~50 m wide is set up. Lastly, 20 m away from the belt, a standing reed fence is set up)

② 芦苇立式栅栏阻沙带(地面以上高度130cm) *Standing reed fence sand barrier belt (130 cm high above ground)*

③ 芦苇行固沙带 *Reed sand barrier belt*

④ 棉花杆方格固沙带 *Cotton bar grid sand barrier belt*

⑤ 稻草帘方格固沙带
Straw grid sand barrier belt

⑥ 编织布方格固沙带　*Geo-synthetic grid sand barrier belt*

图 5.5 中国第一条沙漠铁路—包兰铁路穿越腾格里沙漠南缘。由卵石防火带、灌溉造林带、草障植物带、前缘阻沙带、封沙育草带组成的“五带一体”的治沙防护体系，在沙漠铁路沿线两侧形成一道绿色屏障，被誉为“世界上首位的沙漠治理工程”。（张景光 提供）

Fig 5.5 The first Chinese desert railway- the Baotou-Lanzhou railway - passes through the southern boundary of the Tengger Desert. The sand-protection system, consisting of a pebble fire protection belt, irrigation forestation belt, plants-as-barrier vegetation belt, front sand barrier belt and sand-binding vegetation belt, forms a green barrier on both sides of the railway. This project is known as "the first -ranking desert improvement project in the world". (ZHANG Jingguang)

图 5.6 陕西榆靖高速公路位于毛乌素沙漠南缘，是中国第一条沙漠高速公路。对公路两侧用地范围内的沙漠化土地以“三带（平整带、防护带和保护带）一体”的公路固沙防护体系进行有效防治，路基两侧的防风固沙以植物防护为主。（侯军亭　提供）

Fig 5.6 Situated on the southern boundary of the Mu Us Desert, the Yulin-Jingbian expressway in Shaanxi Province is China's first expressway in desert areas. The desertification on both sides of the expressway has been improved effectively by a highway sand barrier system that consists of a levelling belt, buffer belt and protection belt. On both sides of the roadbed the main sand barrier type is vegetation. (HOU Junting)

图 5.7 内蒙古地区沙漠面积较大，沙漠公路总里程近 5000km。路基防护采用阻、固、输、导综合治理方案，防沙措施主要有：草方格沙障、沙袋沙障、植物活沙障、黏土或砾石沙障、枝条篱笆沙障或栅栏等，并特别注重工程防护与植被防护的有效结合。（燕建民、张建栋 提供）

Fig 5.7 The desert area in the Inner Mongolia Autonomous Region is extensive. The total length of desert highways is close to 5,000 km. A comprehensive scheme has been adopted to protect the roadbed. It can block, bind and transfer sand. The main sand protection measures are: straw grid barriers, sand bag barriers, plant barriers, clay or gravel barriers, branch fences, etc. The effective combination of engineering protection and vegetation protection is emphasized.(YANG Jianmin ,ZHANG Jiandong)

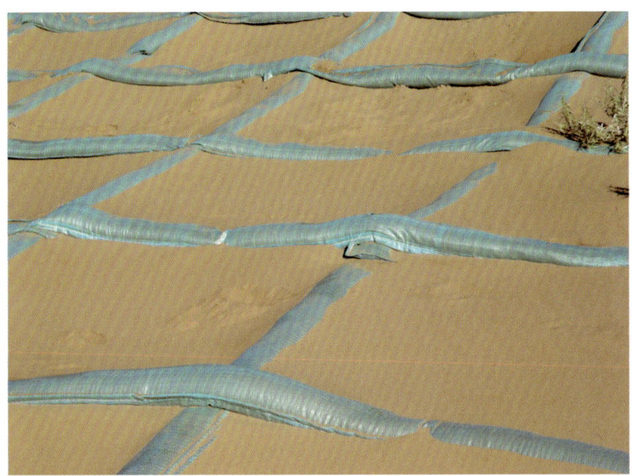

① 无鳍形沙袋沙障 *Sand bag barrier without fins*

② 有鳍形沙袋沙障 *Sand bag barrier with fins*

③ 格状沙袋沙障。用直径 10cm、长 2m 左右的土工布编织袋就地装满流沙，然后在沙丘上摆放成 1m × 1m 的方格。沙袋沙障的每一单元均可移动，因此可根据需要随时调节沙障的规格，沙障被沙埋后还可以重新提起恢复如新。沙袋沙障固定流沙后，可采用植物措施增强固沙效果。

Combination of sand bag barriers and vegetation as protection.Grid-shaped sand bag barriers. Geo-cloth bags 10 cm in diameter and 2 m in length are filled with field sand and laid on sand dunes in 1 m × 1 m grids. Every grid cell is movable and the barriers can be adjusted accordingly. If they are buried by sand, they can be recovered and used anew. After the sand bag barriers have stabilized the mobile sand, vegetation measures can be used to further stabilize the sand.

④ 土工格室沙障　*Geocell barriers*

⑤ 化学喷固沙埂沙障。将流沙堆成一定规格的沙埂，然后用土壤凝结剂固结，以沙治沙。沙障中还可种植各种固沙植物。

Sand baulk barriers solidified by chemical methods: the barriers are formed by moulding mobile sand into standard sand baulks and solidifying the latter with earth coagulator. Inside the barriers many sand-binding plants can be grown.

⑥ 黄柳活沙障固沙（国道207线）：黄柳是浑善达克沙地自然生长的一种先锋灌木，耐干旱贫瘠，抗风蚀、喜沙埋。使用1～2年生的黄柳活枝条，切成60cm的插条，按2～4m见方的规格在流沙上栽插成网格，网格内还可种植白柠条、沙棘、杨柴等当地沙生树木。

Yellow willow sand barriers (along No.207 national highway): the yellow willow tree is a naturally pioneer bush found in Hunshadake Sands. It has strong resistance against arid and barren conditions as well as deflation, and thrives particularly well in sand-covered conditions. The barriers are built by planting 1 to 2-year-old willow branches, each 60 cm long, on mobile sand in 2~4 m cell grids. Inside the grids indigenous psammophytes such as white caragana intermedia, sea backthern and hedysorm leave Maxim can be planted.

■路基边坡防护：工程措施，如黏土包边、土工网垫、平铺碎砾石等；生物措施，如草皮、草方格、三维植物网、植被毯、植生袋等；化学措施，如喷洒乳化沥青、盐液等；综合措施，如网格沙障加种耐旱植物、黏土包边或网格加植物防护、土工网垫植草防护等。

■Roadbed slope protection measures include: engineering measures such as clay cover, earthwork mesh cushion and flat pavement of gravel; plant measures such as sod, straw checkerboard barrier, three demensional plant net, plant cover and biological plant bag; chemical measures such as spraying emulsified asphaltum or salt solution; integrated measures such as grid-shaped sand barrier plus planting drought-resisting vegetation, clay cover or grid plus plant protection, and earthwork mesh cushion plus grass planting protection.

图5.8 内蒙巴吉线路堤边坡采用黏土封闭防护。(张建栋 提供)

Fig 5.8 Clay cover protection technology adopted for a roadbed slope along Bayanhaote-Jilaitai highway in Inner Mongolia. (ZHANG Jiandong)

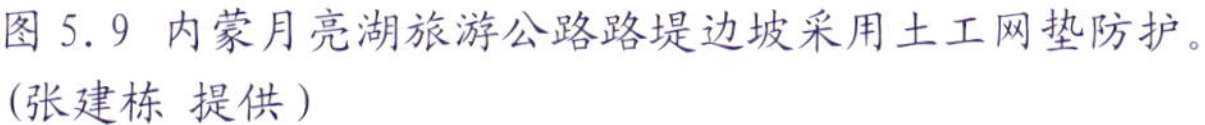

图 5.9 内蒙月亮湖旅游公路路堤边坡采用土工网垫防护。(张建栋 提供)

Fig 5.9 Earthwork mesh cushion protection technology adopted for a roadbed slope along Yueliianghu tourist highway in Inner Mongolia. (ZHANG Jiandong)

图 5.10 内蒙省际通道路堑边坡采用平铺碎砾石。(李涛 摄)

Fig 5.10 Flat pavement of gravel protection technology adopted for a cutting slope along the inter-province highway in Inner Mongolia. (LI Tao)

图 5.11 内蒙阿左旗路堤边坡层铺稻草防护。(张建栋 提供)

Fig 5.11 Rice straw paving protection technology adopted for a roadbed slope along AzhuoQi in Inner Mongolia. (ZHANG Jiandong)

图 5.12 阿拉尔至和田沙漠公路路堑边坡采用方格芦苇边坡防护。芦苇杆长 35cm，其中地下 20cm，地面以上 15cm。(张建军 摄)

Fig 5.12 The Grid-shaped reed bar protection technology is implemented in the cutting slope along the Alaer-Hetian highway. The length of the reed bar is 35 cm, of which a 20 cm section is buried underground. (ZHANG Jianjun)

图 5.13 内蒙赤通高速公路路堤边坡采用生态植被毯防护。(张建栋 提供)

Fig 5.13 Roadbed slope protection with an eco-friendly vegetation carpet along Chifeng-Tongliao expressway in Inner Mongolia. (ZHANG Jiandong)

① 边坡覆盖植被毯

Slope covered with a vegetation carpet

② 边坡植被被成活披绿 *Greening of a slope with vegetation*

图 5.14 内蒙达熬线路堤边坡采用植生袋防护。(张建栋 提供)

Fig 5.14 Biological plant bag protection technology adopted for a roadbed slope along Daao Line in Inner Mongolia. (ZHANG Jiandong)

图 5.15 内蒙省际通道路堑边坡采用网格稻草和植物综合防护。(燕建民 摄)

Fig 5.15 Integrated protection technology of grid-shaped rice straw barriers plus vegetation protection for cutting slope along The inter-province highway in Inner Mongolia .(YAN Jianmin)

① 榆林至陕蒙界高速公路

Shaanxi (Yulin) to Inner Mongolia expressway

② 榆林至靖边高速公路

Yulin to Jingbian expressway

图 5.16 榆靖高速公路、榆蒙高速公路采用稻草沙障、黏土包边、土工网垫等加种紫穗槐或沙柳等旱生植物综合防护路基边坡。(侯军亭 提供)

Fig 5.16 Integrated protection technology combining rice straw barriers, clay cover, earthwork mesh cushion and planting xerophytes (such as amorpha and salix) is implemented in the roadbed slopes along the Yulin-Jingbian expressway and Yulin-Inner Mongolia expressway. (HOU Junting)

附录 中国公路与铁路工程边坡技术创新的代表性机构

APPENDIX Representative Institution for Technological Innovation on Highway & Railway Engineered Slopes

伴随着道路工程建设的快速发展，中国公路与铁路工程边坡研究的理论水平和应用技术水平也不断提升。特别是近几年来，中国交通行业结合山区公路与铁路高边坡病害防治的工程实践，组织技术实力雄厚的勘察、设计、研究单位开展了大量的研究和总结，在取得了一系列具有较高水平的技术创新成果的同时，也造就了一批各具特色的技术创新团队。中交第一公路勘察设计研究院有限公司、中铁西北科学研究院有限公司就是这一创新队伍中的两个典型代表。

Rapid development in road construction in China has also seen a continuous rise in standards in the study of highway and railway engineered slopes both in terms of theoretical research and technical application. This is especially evident in recent years as large quantities of research and findings have come to light as a result of collaboration between transport corporations, which had accumulated copious knowledge in the treatment of highway and railway slopes, and working units armed with sound technological expertise in investigation, design and research. Hence, technological innovations of a high standard aside, many diverse technological organizations have also been nurtured at the same time. Among them, CCCC First Highway Consultants Co., Ltd. and Northwest Research Institute Co,, Ltd of CREC are two representative technological innovation Corporations.

① 边坡（滑坡）勘察 *Site investigation of slope (landslide)*

② 室内模拟试验 *Simulation in lab test*

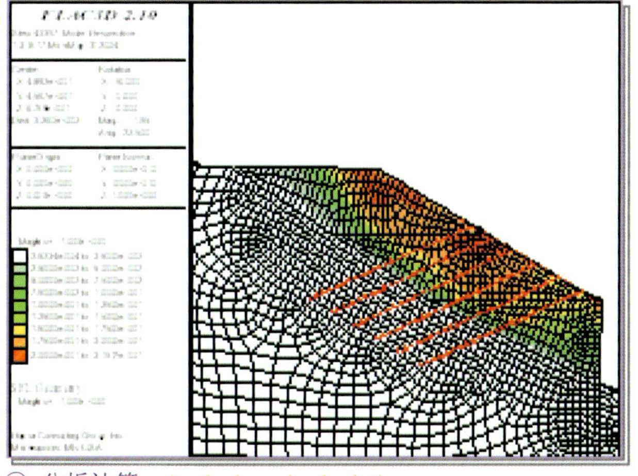

③ 分析计算 *Analysis and calculation*

④ 现场监测 *Field monitoring*

中交第一公路勘察设计研究院有限公司
CCCC First Highway Consultants Co., Ltd.

中交第一公路勘察设计研究院有限公司成立于1952年，是集公路、铁路、市政道路、轨道交通、地质灾害防治等工程的勘察、设计、施工、研究、监理、咨询等于一体的大型综合性咨询企业集团。

山区公路工程综合勘测设计技术和特殊自然环境下的公路建养技术是该院的优势技术领域，尤其是高原多年冻土区公路修筑技术一直占据着行业制高点，总体处于国际领先地位。55年来承担完成了川藏公路、大（同）运（城）高速公路、西（安）汉（中）高速公路、京珠高速公路粤境北段、蒙（自）新（街）河（口）高速公路、福（州）宁（德）高速公路、徽（州）杭（州）高速公路等百余条山区公路沿线高边坡与地质灾害的勘察、设计、研究、咨询、审查以及监测检测和治理工程施工任务，承担了三峡库区武隆滑坡等重大地质灾害防治工程的勘察、设计与咨询，成功处治了诸如川藏公路102滑坡、二郎山滑坡群等著名的特殊复杂边坡工程。主持、参与了"国家干线公路边坡灾害防治"等多项研究课题和《公路工程地质勘察规范》、《公路路线设计规范》等多部行业规范编制工作。在边坡工程综合勘察和处治设计与施工技术等方面积累了丰富的实践经验。

网　　址: www.ccroad.com.cn　　电子邮箱: kjyf@ccroad.com.cn
邮政编码: 710075　　电　　话: 029-88322888
传　　真: 029-88323210　　地　　址: 西安市高新区科技二路63号

Established in 1952, CCCC First Highway Consultants Co., LTD (FHCC) is a comprehensive consulting corporation specializing in surveying, design, construction, supervision and consulting for highway, railway, municipal road, and track communication engineering as well as geological disaster prevention and control.

FHCC's is known for its expertise in comprehensive surveying and design technology for highways in mountainous regions and the construction and maintenance of highways in special natural conditions. It has an international leading edge in construction technique for highways on permanently frozen soil in plateau regions. Over the past 55 years, FHCC has been involved in the survey, design, research, consulting, inspection, monitoring and repair of many highways and expressways. Typical projects include the Sichuan-Tibet Highway, Datong-Yuncheng Expressway, Xi'an-Hanzhong Expressway, Beijing-Zhuhai Expressway, Neimeng-Xingjie-Hekou Expressway, Fuzhou-Ningde Expressway, Huizhou-Hangzhou Expressway. It was also responsible for the survey, design and consultancy for major disaster prevention projects, namely the Wulong landslide project in the Three Gorges area. It has also diagnosed and treated with success a number of well-known landslides, such as the No.102 landslide on the Sichuan-Tibet highway, and Erlangshan landslides. FHCC has also overseen, and participated in, research projects such as 'Slope disaster prevention and control on national highways and expressways', and the compilation of industry codes such as 'Codes for geological investigation on highways', 'Design codes for highway road lines'. FHCC has accumulated a wealth of experience in slope engineering regarding comprehensive surveying, treatment plans and construction techniques.

Web Site : www.ccroad.com.cn　　E-mail : kjyf@ccroad.com.cn
Post Coad : 710075　　Tel : 029-88322888
Fax:029-88323210　　ADD : No.63 Keji 2nd Road, Xi'an , China

中铁西北科学研究院有限公司

Northwest Research Institute Co., Ltd of CREC

中铁西北科学研究院有限公司成立于1961年，是集科学研究、工程咨询、勘察设计、工程检测与监测等为一体并取得ISO9001质量认证的综合性科技型企业。近半个世纪以来，以特殊地质路基与地质灾害防治的重大应用理论及灾害防治措施研究为主攻方向，紧密结合铁路、交通和地质灾害防治领域开展科学研究与技术创新，取得包括国家自然科学奖、省部级科技奖在内的科技成果近300项，先后成功地为中国基础设施建设完成了2000余项地质灾害防治工程。

滑坡与高边坡病害防治是该院的重要专业，深入系统地研究了滑坡的发生和发展规律以及新型防治措施，取得了包括滑坡的综合分类与分布规律、滑坡稳定性分析评价和推力计算方法，黏性滑带土的强度特性、残余抗剪强度变化规律，以及滑坡与高边坡病害的空间预测与时间预报理论和方法，抗滑桩的设计理论和方法等一系列成果。

该院拥有著名滑坡专家徐邦栋、王恭先研究员，并形成以69名高级技术人员为核心的滑坡防治研究的人才队伍，拥有国内先进的大型滑坡机理和结构试验室，为中国科协咨询中心滑坡防治专家委员会挂靠单位。先后出版《滑坡分析与防治》等20部专著，主编《滑坡分析与文集》，其中《滑坡防治》一书是中国第一部滑坡的专著。

Founded in 1961, and a holder of the ISO 9001 quality authentication, Northwest Research Institute is a comprehensive technological enterprise specializing in scientific research, engineering consultancy, survey and design, engineering testing and monitoring. Over the past 50 years, the institute has engaged in applied research on special geological road bases and geological disaster control and the relevant measures, in close conjunction with research and innovations in the field of railway, communication and geological disaster control. For its work, it has received nearly 300 research awards, including the National Award for the Natural Sciences and the Provincial Award for Technology. It has completed a total of over 2,000 disaster prevention projects for the infrastructure in China.

One major expertise of the institute is landslide and high slope disaster control. Its rigorous and systematic study of the occurrence, development patterns and new control measures of landslides has yielded numerous results: a comprehensive classification of landslides and their distribution patterns, stability analysis evaluation of landslide and thrust calculation methods, the strength feature of cohesive soil in slide zones, laws of variation of residual shear strength, theories and methods of space and time forecast of landslide and high slope disasters, and design theory and method of antiskid piles.

The institute comprises 69 senior technologists who are its core members, among whom Professor Xu Bangdong and research fellow Wang Gongxian are renowned landslide experts. It boasts an advanced large^{a2}scale landslide mechanism and structure laboratory, and administers the Landslide Control Expert Committee of the Consulting Centre of the China Science Society. The institute has published more than 20 monographs, including Landslide Analysis and Its Control, which is the first landslide monograph in China, and edited the journal of Proceeding of Landslide.

(Web Site):www.ztxbkxyjy.com (E-mail):zgztxby@163.com
(Post Coad):730000 (Tel):0931-4934554 (Fax):0931-4934524
ADD: 365 East Minzhu Road, Lanzhou , China

致 谢

本画册在编写过程中始终得到交通部专家委员会凤懋润主任、中国科学院陈祖煜院士的指导和支持。牛富俊、王学军、喻林青、姜献民、焦臣、罗满良、杨晓华等同志参与了部分调研和编辑工作。

为本画册提供资料的主要单位有：西安中交公路岩土工程有限责任公司、江苏省交通规划设计院有限公司、长安大学、陕西省公路勘察设计院、新疆交通科学研究院、中国科学院沙坡头治沙站、内蒙古交通设计研究院有限责任公司、陕西交通报社、西汉高速公路公司、重庆交通科研设计院、西藏自治区交通科学研究所、铁道第一勘察设计院、铁道第二勘察设计院、黑龙江交通科学研究所、武汉中财科技有限公司等。

为本画册提供资料信息的主要人员有：王学军、韩文宪、牛富俊、喻林青、鲁安新、朱聪功、王传仁、倪万魁、路勋、刘涛、姜献民、张建栋、燕建民、张景光、李高旺、焦臣、张正波、张建军、杨晓华、张玉芳、李安洪、李响、邓卫东、张永刚、侯军亭、张琼、赵刚、唐良健、石剑欣、李涛、刘卫民等。

在此对所有相关单位、人员和支持本书出版的专家和同志表示衷心感谢！

Acknowledgements

Special thanks to FENG Maorun, director of expert committee in Ministry of communications, and CHEN Zuyu, academician of the Chinese Academy of Sciences for their guide and support. Also thanks to NIU Fujun, WANG Xuejun, YU Linqing, JIANG Xianmin, JIAO Chen, LUO Manliang, YANG Xiaohua who took part in investigation and editing.

Thanks to Xi'an China Highway Geotechnical Engineering Co., LTD, Jiangsu Traffic Planning and Design Research Institute Co., LTD, Chang'an University, Shaanxi Highway Design Institute, XinJiang Science Research Institute of Communications, Shapotou Trial Station of the Chinese Academy of Sciences, Inner Mongolia Communications Design and Research Institute Co., LTD, Shaanxi Communication Newspaper, Xihan Expressway Company, Chongqing Communications Research and Design Institute, Tibet Communications Research and Design Institute, The First Survey & Design Institute of China Railways, Second Survey and Design Institute of China Railways, Heilongjiang Communications Research and Design Institute, Wuhan Zhongcai Science & Technology Co., Ltd for their assistance in providing valuable material.

Also thanks to WANG Xuejun, HAN Wenxian, NIU Fujun, YUN Linqing, LU Anxin, ZHU Conggong, WANG Chuanren, NI Wankui, LU Xun, LIU Tao, JIANG Xianmin, ZHANG Jiandong, YAN Jianmin, ZHANG Jingguang, LI Gaowang, JIAO Chen, ZHANG Zhengbo, ZHANG Jianjun, YANG Xiaohua, ZHANG Yufang, LI Anhong, LI Xiang, DENG Weidong, ZHANG Yonggang, HOU Junting, ZHANG Qiong, ZHAO Gang, TANG Liangjian, SHI Jianxin, LI Tao, LIU Weimin for their assistance in providing valuable information.